Jessi is an independent woman who graduated from the Minneapolis College of Art and Design. She has been working in advertising for over 10 years, where it's very (white) male-dominated. She's here to break barriers and comfort zones. Jessi tries to host fundraisers for rescue dogs as often as possible. While being one of "those" millennial dog moms – which she's very proud of.

Am I allowed to thank Chelsea Handler here? I'm going to do it. As my main influence and inspiration thank you Chelsea for breaking barriers ahead of me.

My friends, my loved ones, my loved friends, dogs, ex-lovers, my family – you've all made this possible by, well, making me who I am.

Jessi Aylward

# And I'm Only 30

Austin Macauley Publishers™

LONDON * CAMBRIDGE * NEW YORK * SHARJAH

**Ordering Information**
Quantity sales: Special discounts are available on quantity purchases by corporations, associations, and others. For details, contact the publisher at the address below.

**Publisher's Cataloging-in-Publication data**
Aylward, Jessi
And I'm Only 30

ISBN 9798889105947 (Paperback)
ISBN 9798889105961 (ePub e-book)
ISBN 9798889105954 (Audiobook)

Library of Congress Control Number: 2023920047

www.austinmacauley.com/us

First Published 2024
Austin Macauley Publishers LLC
40 Wall Street, 33rd Floor, Suite 3302
New York, NY 10005 USA

mail-usa@austinmacauley.com
+1 (646) 5125767

In no particular order: Rita / Tara, Sara, Sarah & Luke, Claribel, Momo, Colie, Tiffany, Beck, Fenix, Eileen, Juliana, Marv (and all the gays/girlies), Anastasia, Antoinette, Celina, Shelley, Margaret, Gen, Mal, Mel, Roe, Reb, Mary, Vicky, Juliana, Akuro, Ryan, TJ, Keith, Katie, Danni / Adrienne, Anita and those who better make me acknowledge you by the time And I'm only 35 comes out! To you all, you have been a rock during my self-induced sandstorm. Thank you.

Joab – don't you dare ever change!

# Prologue

There had been times when I had flirted with the bottom of the barrel. Maybe I had even put a single foot on the bottom, but I've always been able to make my way back to the top, or at least the middle. When I broke up with Jamie, I lay on the bottom of the barrel and didn't come up for a long time.

Jamie was one of the first guys to break up with me. He probably wasn't even the best guy I had broken up with. Why, then, did I fall into such a deep depression? I could barely get out of bed, work, or walk my dog, Buttercup.

For years, with the stress of work and the roller coaster of dating, I was able to square my shoulders, take a deep breath, and move on. I had to. What else was I going to do?

Sure, I knew that there was probably something wrong with me. I was the first to admit it. Work was stressful – I was a woman working in advertising. "Stressful" barely scratched the surface.

Growing up as a millennial in the shadow of war, of recession, of climate change, I thought my anxiety was just something everyone else in my generation experienced.

But then Jamie and I broke up.

On our first date, we went to a new bar in Bushwick. I tried hard to find a bar that my friends wouldn't frequent.

My friends are amazing, but they can be a lot when they've had a few drinks, and I wanted Jamie to myself.

It was six o'clock on a Tuesday. The weather was perfect. I didn't worry about sweating through my light top, picked to perfectly accentuate my eyes. I walked down the street, knowing he would be there before I was. Buttercup strutted confidently on a leash in front of me. I had barely taken off my sunglasses when I saw him. He had gorgeous eyes, the kind that pull you in and mesmerize you. I was fascinated by his eyes from the beginning. The tattoos on his arms accentuated his muscles. The piercings in his ears and eyebrows gave him an edge that was very attractive. He was tall, pale, and looked like a lost puppy. I've always loved dogs.

We greeted each other, then Jamie grabbed the drinks he had purchased from the bar, and we moved to the back patio since I had Buttercup.

"Tell me more about what kind of producing you do?" Jamie asked me.

"Two years after I moved to New York, I worked at HBO."

"Like Game of Thrones?"

I laughed. "Not quite. I did some campaign ads, but never the big fish. I wish, though!"

"How long were you there?" he asked.

"Not as long as I wanted. I was covering a mat leave, so only six months."

"How's your drink?"

"Oh, it's great, thanks." He wasn't looking at me anymore. He focused on something behind me. I turned around to see what he saw. "Is there something…"

"Sorry, it just looked like someone was pointing at you."
I had to shift to see beyond another patron's head but didn't see anything out of the ordinary. I shifted back in my seat.

"I mean; it wouldn't be out of the realm of possibility. I'm pretty sure 75% of my friends live in Bushwick." A dog barked, which I would usually ignore, but right after I heard the dog bark, I felt a tingle of premonition.

Jamie must have noticed. "Don't tell me you can recognize a dog bark?"

"No. I mean, I'm sure I could hear Buttercup bark in a group of a hundred dogs, but that's it."

I heard the dog bark again, and this time I looked in the direction of the sound. I saw the dog and groaned. "I do know that dog." I also knew the person holding the dog's leash and the five other people with them. I quickly whipped around. "I promise; I did not plan this. Please do not hold this against me!"

Jamie laughed and petted the dog that had rushed up to greet Buttercup.

"That's Rosie." I wasn't going to introduce my friends. It wasn't Rosie's fault; she was just a dog. My friends could take the damn hint and leave. I glared at all of them, but especially Dee, who was Rosie's owner.

"Hi, I'm Dee," she said, and pointedly ignored me. She offered her hand to Jamie to shake.

"This is Jamie," I said. "We are having our first drink ever in real life." I heavily emphasized the latter part of my sentence.

"Nice to meet you!" Dee could see the hint I was throwing her way. She just refused to take it.

"Why are you here?" I tried. "We never come here."

"We're going to Old Stanley's, but we wanted to try something new before we went, and this was the closest. Why don't you come with us?"

I could have died. No, I could have made sure Dee died. At least Jamie didn't look upset. "Thanks, but we're good here. Maybe next time."

I held my breath, unsure if Dee would insist we join them, but she finally took the hint, and they went on their way. I held my breath, but I didn't want Jamie to know how much my friend's arrival had affected me, so I slowly and silently blew the air out of my mouth.

"I swear to everything I did not plan that," I said.

"It's fine. I promised my parents a walk-by too."

I was bringing the glass to my lips when he said that, and I froze for a moment. "You're joking."

He laughed. "I am."

Okay, maybe it was the first time we met in real life, but I knew then that he was the first man I could see myself in a relationship with. He could be more than a booty call. More than a one-night stand. More than what I'd had before.

We eventually finished our drinks – something neither of us rushed. I toyed with the idea of asking if we should order something to eat. I wanted to spend more time with him, but I had made a promise to myself that I wouldn't sleep with anyone on the first date anymore.

"I have to go to work early tomorrow, but let me walk you to Old Stanley's, and you can meet up with your friends."

"Are you sure?"

"Of course. This way we get to talk a little longer." Jamie paid the bill. Normally I would have a fairly brisk pace, but with Jamie, I held back a bit. I wanted to spend as much time with him as I could. Our fingers interlaced as we talked about Buttercup and the next time we were going to meet.

Just past the group of smokers outside Old Stanley, we stopped. "I had fun," I said.

"Same."

He put his arms around my waist, and I put my arms around his shoulders. I knew the smokers wouldn't care, and no one walking the New York City streets would think twice about two people making out on the sidewalk, so I leaned into it, his tongue dancing with mine, his arms tightening around me, and mine tightening around him.

"Woo, Jess!" I heard Dee yell. Moment ruined.

"Thanks, Dee," I called back. "Bye, Jamie. Text me when you're back."

"You bet. See ya." I watched Jamie walk down the street before I joined my friends. "You are all assholes!" I said. They all laughed in response, then bought me a drink.

Jamie and I were inseparable for three months – or as inseparable as we could be with demanding jobs. I often worked late, and as a second chef, he was at work early, but we did what we could to spend time together.

"Do you want to come to my birthday party?" Jamie asked me out of the blue when we were smoking outside, watching Buttercup smell the weeds poking up from the cracks in the sidewalk.

"Of course," I said. *This was really going somewhere. I'd meet his friends, and we'd have a real-life, grown-up relationship.*

His favorite candy bar was Kit Kat, so I made a two-tier chocolate cake with Kit Kats lining the edge as a surprise. I might not be a second chef, but I nailed that cake. I, however, did not nail the taxi ride there. I had gone out the night before and drank without consideration for the following day– my favorite way to drink and even though it had been hours since I woke up, my hangover hit hard.

"Pull over," I groaned to the cabbie.

"We're not there yet."

"Pull over!"

The cabbie pulled over, and I barely had enough time to open the door and vomit onto the curb. I had the presence of mind to make sure the cake was far enough away from me that there would be no way for anything to happen to it. There was a moment when I wondered if I should just go home, but it was Jamie's birthday. I could get it together for him. He deserved to be celebrated. The cabbie wasn't happy, but he continued to the bar with only a few glares at me in the rear-view mirror, which I ignored.

I arrived later than I expected, but I was early enough to have some one-on-one time with Jamie's closest friends. I saw how much Jamie was loved by his friends. *This is a good guy,* I told myself, watching him embrace everyone who came over to wish him well.

"Babe!" he said at the bar when I presented him with the cake. All his friends oohed and awed over it before cutting it and passing it around. "This is incredible." His friends smothered me with hugs and admiration for the cake. Jamie didn't pay for a single drink that night, and I quickly caught up to the rest of them.

I had another engagement that night, and I didn't want to be clingy and get in the way of Jamie spending time with his friends on his birthday, so I kissed Jamie goodbye and told him I'd see him soon. The next morning, despite an extreme hangover, I was happy. Jamie made me so happy, and I couldn't believe I had finally found someone who could make me feel this way.

Then our schedules seemed to catch up to us. Once, we would have made sure we texted if we couldn't see each other for a while, but Jamie became radio silent for long stretches. I was annoyed, but I also knew that he was busy and I was busy. Was there any point in bringing it up if there really was no good solution? I didn't talk to him about it, but I didn't become any less annoyed.

At least my friend's BBQ was coming up, and he had promised to come to that. It seemed only fair, since I had met his friends, that he met mine. We hadn't had run-ins as we had with Dee on our first date. He promised he was going to come, and I planned to hold him to it. There had been too many broken dates already.

I went to the BBQ on my own because Jamie was working in the morning. He was going to meet me after his shift. I wasn't going to wait for Jamie to have fun, so I was drinking freely and accepting hits of the drugs being offered. When I got a text notification on my phone, I assumed it would be him telling me he was on his way. Instead, he was telling me he had changed his mind that he wasn't going to come. Rough shift, and he still had an hour to go.

Not gonna make bbq.

I deflated. Did he ever have any intention of coming, or did he put me through the paces knowing he was going to bail on my friends and me? I drank more and took more drugs. Then I sent him a text when I knew his shift was over.

Jamie pls. You prmisd. Jst come 4 a bit.

No. Tired.

One drink?

No.

Can I come over and see u?

No.

"Sofia!" I yelled. "Sofia!"

"I'm literally right beside you," Sofia responded to my right.

"Take my phone," I said. "Jamie is pissing me off, and I don't want to say anything I'm going to regret."

I thought I had saved the situation. I made sure that the disagreement didn't get out of hand. Jamie called me the next morning. "Hey. You good?"

"A little hungover, but I'm okay. I wish you could have come."

"I know. Look, I don't think this is working out."

"What?"

"Our schedules, you know."

"That's bullshit. We were making it work. Is this because I wanted you to come to the party? Because you promised. It wasn't cool that you bailed at the last minute."

"I don't want to get into a fight."

"So we're not even going to talk about it?"

"There's nothing to talk about," he said. "It's over."

The floor ceased to exist. How was I standing? Was I even standing? Did I remember how to breathe? Where was my emotional support dog, Buttercup?

What had happened? He was someone I saw a future with. Why didn't he see a future with me? Were the broken parts of me that obvious? Maybe I couldn't hide it as well as I thought. Maybe there was too much damage.

I turned off my bedroom light and curled into a tight ball on my bed. Hello, bottom of the barrel, I'm Jess, and I'm going to be your host for the rest of my life.

# And I'm Only in High School

The first time I kissed a boy was after a football game. He and I walked behind my friend and her sister through the parking lot. Our team had won, and all around us were celebrating fans and players. The air was charged with excitement. He squeezed my hand tighter as we drew nearer to the spot we were to meet our ride.

"Are you cold?" he asked.

"I'm fine," I said, but I walked closer to him, so our shoulders touched. He was warmer than I was, and his warmth spread across my upper body.

When I was young, I called myself a nerd. I loved to study and would always read ahead in assignments. Homework didn't bother me as much as it bothered my classmates because I enjoyed it. When schoolwork was done, it was time to play video games, read, or even watch horror movies. My dad is a psychologist, and my mom never grew out of the hippie lifestyle of the late 60s and early 70s, so while some of my friends had hard and fast rules about almost everything, mom and dad gave me the space to explore. Even though they didn't give me strict boundaries and I found myself hiding behind a computer screen, pretending I was an expert on sexting in anonymous chatrooms, I still avoided uncomfortable situations. I was hyper-aware when romantic and sexual scenes came on the TV screen while watching films and shows with my parents. I squirmed and tried to look anywhere, while my parents didn't think anything was amiss.

My life was unfiltered, thanks to my parents, but at the same time, I wasn't running out to have the random sexual encounters I read about in the chat rooms. I still knew I needed some kind of connection, even if I didn't necessarily know what that connection should be. I couldn't define it, but did I need to define it?

I grew up in a small town in Minnesota with short summers and harsh winters. I knew that I wouldn't spend my entire life in Minnesota. I dreamed of New York City: the lights, the people, the buildings, and the opportunities. But I wasn't in New York yet. I was in high school with my boyfriend Adam and my friends Shelly, Amber, and Lisa.

I hadn't known Adam for long. In our town, the high school merged two middle schools together. And the summer between junior and senior year, I met Adam. Somehow, we had not crossed paths in three years in a small high school town. He was safe, kind, and easy going.

I met him at a friend's house just before Senior year started. My friend's mother announced a game of Pin the Tail on the Donkey, and I got way too excited. I opened the door to the basement where the game was to be held, and the door swung back and struck me in the face. Before I knew it, I was lying down on the couch with Adam looking down at me and holding ice to my forehead. Fast forward to a movie date night; we were sitting in the car park after our movie just chatting the two of us. When he very nervously asked, "Do you want to be my girlfriend?" Which I was excited for but didn't respond as such with just a "Sure" and giggle. So that was that – I had my first official boyfriend.

"What are you doing tomorrow?" he asked one day at school as we stood waiting between classes, my friend and her sister giving us space. I knew they could still see and hear us, but I appreciated the gesture. The sun began its slow descent, casting rays of rose gold across the sky, welcoming the moon. The stars dimly twinkled above, providing the perfect ambiance for the moment.

I shrugged. "I have math homework. Not that I want to do it."

"I could come over and help."

I laughed. "Do you even know what Mr. Chews Gum While Speaking is talking about half the time?" Shelly had been caught with notes during the first test, and when she raged about him after her detention, the name stuck.

"Actually, I do. Seriously. Maybe I should be a mathematician when I grow up," he said.

"No, you're supposed to be in a band, and I'm going to be your groupie girlfriend. Like Penny Lane in *Almost Famous.*"

"I don't think things worked out with her so well."

"I said like her, not the same as." There weren't as many fans in the parking lot as five minutes earlier. Cars were emptying out, but we were still waiting. "If you want to come over and help, then I want you to. My parents will be home."

"I like your parents." Everyone liked my parents. They were always the most laid-back of my friends' parents.

"Okay. So, tomorrow?" I turned my chin up. He wasn't that much taller than me; my forehead matched up with his nose.

"Tomorrow," he murmured. We stood there in an awkward tableau. I wanted him to kiss me. What was he waiting for? I shifted a little closer, and then I put my arms around him. His arms went around my upper back, and he moved me even closer to him. My head tipped back, and I saw his eyes close slightly as his head came even closer to mine. I closed my eyes and waited for the touch of his lips.

They were warmer than I had expected. And softer. I had thought his lips would be dry, but they were as moist as mine. His tongue hesitantly touched my closed lips, and I opened them. My tongue met his, and they danced together for a moment. His hands grazed the top of my butt, and I wrapped my arms tighter around his back. Then, almost as if we had both agreed, we pulled back. He smiled at me, and I smiled back.

A car horn honked while we were engulfed in a light beam. I pulled away. "Oh, my God." I wasn't expecting this first kiss with him to have an audience!

"I should go," Adam said. He wasn't at all perturbed at our exposure. If anything, he seemed proud.

I took another step backward. I desperately wanted to look at his crotch. I wanted to see if the kiss did anything to him. I had read so many stories that had that first kiss as the moment that turned them both on enough that sex came right after. Was that true with every first kiss?

"Jess, come on!" my friend yelled. "Either get in or get a room."

"Shelly, oh my God!" I yelled back before sprinting forward and settling in the backseat of the car. I refused to meet anyone's gaze. I waved discreetly to Adam as we passed him.

"Did you have a good time?" Shelly's dad asked.

"Yeah, Jess, did you have a good time?" Shelly's said.

I refused to say another word the entire way back home.

I had no idea how close I could feel to another person. As chill as my parents were and as open as our conversations had always been, there was something missing. With Adam, I had the openness I had with my parents, the friendship I had with my besties, and that physical closeness. It made me feel alive and powerful. I never had that feeling hanging out with the girls or any other friends. I definitely didn't feel like that when it was just my parents and me. I loved that feeling. I wanted that feeling all the time. The next three weeks were spent expanding our boundaries. We quickly mastered making out and moved on to exciting new firsts. Shelly, Amber, Lisa, and I scoured Cosmo magazines to learn more than we learned in health class. If Cosmo said I should give my man a hickey, then Adam would wear a turtleneck after I saw him.

I had just finished sucking on his neck and examined my artwork like a top appraiser. We sat on the edge of his bed. He had iTunes open on his laptop, which sat on his tiny desk, though I couldn't recognize any of the songs. Our shoes had been kicked off and were lying haphazardly on his brown carpet. He slid his fingers into my unbuttoned jeans. The thrill was exhilarating. His mom wasn't home when we came home from school, and neither of us knew what time she'd be back.

I squirmed. "Your hands are cold."

"Sorry," Adam brought out his fingers and blew on them, then continued his journey. "How's that?"

I leaned back on my elbows and looked up at the poster of Eminem on his wall. "It's fine," I breathed. I was pretty sure he was fingering me. I had read the phrase in Cosmo and had seen jokes and other stories online, but I couldn't imagine what it was like then. Now that it was happening to me, I realized that unless I had experienced it, there was no way I could have understood.

When we read Cosmo together, usually in my bedroom huddled together on my queen-sized bed since I had the coveted magazine, Amber's face always went beet red, and she squeezed the yellow pillow that clashed with my purple bedspread. She giggled along with the rest of us, but we all knew her parents were far stricter than even Lisa's, whose grandparents were missionaries. Amber had never kissed a guy, and when we would play truth or dare, she never chose dare. So when I read the story a reader had submitted about her boyfriend fingering her, Amber grew uncomfortable. "How do they fit?" she asked.

"The fingers?" Shelly was looking over my shoulder.

"Yeah. How does anything fit in there?"

"It's not sewed shut." I laughed. "Weren't you there when we talked about tampons in health class?"

"I don't wear tampons," Amber said. "We don't have any in the house."

"You don't? They're so much better than pads. At least you don't have to sit in your blood like a baby in a diaper," Lisa chimed in.

"But tampons give you a toxic shock."

"That's only if you don't change them enough," I said.

"Okay, but a tampon is smaller than a finger."

Shelly, Lisa, and I laughed. "Amber, a baby comes out of there. I'm pretty sure a finger or two won't hurt you."

"Well, it might hurt at first." Lisa looked around at us. "Until the hymen is broken."

"I heard Stacy Mitts broke her hymen when she fell out of a tree," Shelly said. "Or at least that's what she told her boyfriend."

"No, it can happen," I told them. "My mom told me. She said that women weren't supposed to ride bicycles in the olden days because the men told them it would break their hymen, and then they wouldn't be pure. Since we're way more liberated now, most of us have probably done it without realizing." I knew I was parroting Mom but felt it was important my friends knew. "Men have always been using sex to reign in women since forever. We shouldn't be ashamed for liking it. Men aren't."

"I still don't think I'd like fingers in there," Amber said.

When Adam put his fingers in me, I remembered Amber saying she didn't think she'd want to experience this, and I knew she'd change her mind the second it happened to her. I didn't want him to ever take them out. He flicked my button – the clitoris, I reminded myself; if I'm having sex, or at least if I'm sex adjacent, I should be able to think the words, and I gasped and squirmed. The feeling was so overwhelming that I didn't know what to do. It didn't hurt, but it was insistent. He rubbed his finger along it again, and I closed my eyes, biting my lip.

The door down the hall slammed. "Adam! I'm home!"

Adam tore his hands away from me and wiped his fingers on his jeans. I scrambled to do up the zipper and button of my jeans as Adam's mom walked down the hallway. She opened the door and stuck her head in her room. "Adam, can you help me with – oh, hi Jess," she frowned. "Doors are open when you have Jess here, remember?"

"Sorry, Mom," Adam mumbled. "The wind closed it, I think."

She raised an eyebrow, not missing anything. "Uh huh. Well, come on and help me unload the groceries. Are you staying for dinner, Jess?"

"If that's alright with you?" I said, hoping I sounded as normal as possible.

"You're always welcome here. You know that."

After supper, Adam and I went downstairs into the bonus room to watch a movie. We sat on either side of the couch while the opening credits for Burn *After Reading* showed on the TV.

Adam's mom came downstairs and handed us a big bag of chips and two sodas. "I'm going to Sarah's for her Tupperware party. Be back in a few hours."

The second we heard the front door close, Adam launched over at me and pinned me on the couch, sticking his tongue in my mouth. I moaned and rubbed my hands over his back. I could feel him getting hard. Finally, this was just like a Cosmo story. I knew exactly what to do because I had read so many accounts of encounters just like this one. He pushed up my shirt and pulled my breasts out of my bra.

"I can take my bra off," I told him. He was licking one of my nipples and pinching the other one while my breasts hung over my bra.

He nodded, and I pulled off my shirt and reached around to unhook my bra. He stared at my breasts like he had never seen them before. We had already done a lot of under-the-bra sessions, but tonight was different. He grabbed the neck of his shirt and yanked it over his head. He wasn't well-defined, unlike the men in the underwear ads, but he was still hot. I loved looking at his naked chest. I lay down, and he buried his head between my breasts again. I arched my back a bit and played with his hair. This was what the women did in all the movies I had seen.

His hands found my button and my zipper, and I thought I should reciprocate the action. He came up for air, and I took the opportunity to pull down my pants, but Adam needed to pull them off my feet. *Next time I do this*, I told myself, *I'm not going to wear skinny jeans.*

There we were, both fully naked for the first time, in front of each other. "Are you ready?" Adam asked. Before I could respond, he got an alarmed look on his face.

"What?" I turned around, half expecting to see his mom walking in on us.

"I forgot a condom." He reached into his discarded jeans, took his wallet from the back pocket, and pulled out a small square. "Thank fuck." He sighed.

"Do you want me to?" I asked, hoping he would say no.

"No, I've practiced," Adam said without thinking. He paused, the package between his front teeth. "I mean-"

"As long as you know how to do it." I shrugged. I watched, fascinated, as he put the condom on the tip of his penis and rolled the rest of it down his shaft. "That doesn't seem so hard," I said.

Adam whipped up his head. "What?" His shoulders and his penis drooped a little.

"I mean, putting the condom on!" I clarified. Then, for good measure, I reached out and caressed his penis, restoring it to its previous glory.

Adam gently pushed me back onto the couch, his hand cupping my vagina. "Are you wet?"

I nodded. "Do it."

I clenched a little as his penis entered me. There was a little resistance, but we were both persistent and soon he was all the way inside. "Don't move!" He instructed, breathless.

This was much different than having a tampon inside me. I had to tell the girls this. He had told me not to move, but I wanted to feel more than I was feeling. I wanted to shake, I wanted to feel the friction I had felt just before he stopped. Everything felt so good, but at the same time, I knew I could feel better. "Don't move," he whispered again, pinching my nipple and making me gasp loudly. I could feel my Kegels constricting. "What are you doing?" he asked.

"I didn't do anything."

"You did something down there."

"Are you going to do something?" I asked, trying to stay still but wanting so much more.

"Yeah, just give me a second." He took a breath, drew out a bit, then slammed into me with more force than I expected. "Sorry."

"No, it's okay. Do that again, but faster."

I clutched his shoulders as he pumped in and out, both of us out of breath within the first two pumps.

"I'm going to come. Are you going to come?" He could barely talk.

"No, I'm not. Can you wait?"

Adam cried out in a strangled tone, pumped spasmodically for half a minute, then lay against me. He was covered in sweat. "I'm sorry, I couldn't wait."

"Oh!" I said. "Well, that's okay." I had read about this in Cosmo too. "Maybe you could finger me?"

He nodded. "I just need to catch my breath."

Once he pulled out of me and got rid of the condom, he rejoined me on the couch. He moved his fingers around my clitoris and, with my urging, squeezed my nipples. It took longer than he took, but finally, my legs clenched, and everything stopped for a second. He didn't stop rubbing my clitoris, and I had to push his hand away, the feeling of completion bringing with it extreme sensitivity.

"Holy fuck, that was amazing," I said, laughing. Maybe I shouldn't have laughed; maybe I should have marked the occasion with more seriousness, but my emotions were all jumbled up in the best possible way. I felt like I could run a marathon, ace a test, or anything. I knew that everyone said that sex changed everything, and I think I understood why. It changed the way I felt about myself. I was no longer a little girl who wanted to be part of the world. I was the world! "And now I'm thirsty."

"We have soda down here."

I shook my head. "I need water." I put my clothes back on and stood in front of him. "How's my sex hair?"

I ran lightly up the carpeted stairs, which led directly into the kitchen. Opening the cupboard drawer that housed the cups, I called over my shoulder. "Do you want water too, lover boy?"

Adam yelled for me to bring him a cup, and I took two small cups out of the cupboard and closed the door, almost screaming when I saw Adam's mom on the other side. "Sorry, I didn't mean to scare you!" she said.

"No, it's okay. It's good for the heart." I laughed, then remembered my rat's nest of hair. She turned the cold water tap on but didn't move away from the sink.

"How's the movie?" she asked.

"The movie?" I repeated.

"Weren't you two watching a movie?"

"Yeah, we were," my mind raced, trying to remember through the fog of sex what movie we were supposed to have been watching. I knew this. There was George Clooney and Brad Pitt! "Oh, yeah, *Burn After Reading*. It's not bad. Not really my thing, but whatever." I felt smart like I had avoided a trick in a labyrinth.

"And you didn't like the soda? Or maybe you drank it already?" Adam's mom had an innocent look on her face, but there was something about how she was asking the questions that worried me. She knew. I don't know how, but she knew.

"The bubbles were making me burp." I forced a laugh.

"Uh huh. Well, you better get down there; don't want to miss anything." She moved away from the sink so I could fill both cups with water.

"Right. Thanks." I refused to look over my shoulder as I left the kitchen. Looking over my shoulder would have made me look guilty.

"What took you so long?" Adam reached up and took a glass from me. I put mine on the table beside the couch, then collapsed beside him.

"Your mom was there," I moaned. "I think she knew. Does it look that obvious?"

Adam looked at me. "Your hair is kind of…" he trailed off.

I buried my head in my hands. "Oh my god. She's going to tell my parents."

"Like your parents will care."

"They're not completely without rules." A thought terrified me. "Oh my god, they'd probably want to talk about it. In detail!"

"It'll be fine. My mom loves you. And it's not like we're the first seventeen-year-olds to have sex."

"She's never going to let me back in the house. I hope you memorized my body because you're probably never going to see it again."

We watched the rest of the movie in silence, but I was too wrapped up in my embarrassment to be able to follow any of the plot. Plus, we had missed the first twenty minutes or so with our escapade.

"Do you want to watch something else?" Adam asked me when the credits rolled.

"I kind of just want to go home and pretend this didn't happen." Too late, I noticed Adam's hurt face. "No, not everything. That was good. Just the part where your mom knows."

"Jess, I promise it'll be fine. It's not a big deal."

Adam was right. Despite my fears of my parents greeting me with a "You Had Sex for the First Time" party, they welcomed me home like they had dozens of times before. The next time I went over to Adam's house, his mom directed me to his room, where he was waiting for me. I took off my backpack and tossed it on his bed, then realized Adam's mom had followed me down the hall and had quietly closed the bedroom door. I met Adam's eyes.

"Seriously?" I whispered.

"I told you," he said, taking my backpack off the bed and guiding me to lie down on his plaid bedspread. "She loves you."

When I told the girls about Adam and me at our next Cosmo session in my room with Sally, my dog, lounging in her bed by my door, they all squealed, even Amber. "You've lost your virginity," she said.

Thanks to my parents' well-rounded discussions around the dinner table, I had never used the phrase "lost my virginity" before. It wasn't like a key or my mom's favorite earrings that I swore I wouldn't lose but then did. I knew exactly where it went. And I was definitely more upset about losing my mom's earrings than I was about having sex with Adam. I'm pretty sure my mom would say the same thing. I didn't tell the girls this, and I certainly didn't tell Adam, but I would have had sex with whomever I was dating. I just happened to be dating Adam. It's not like Adam wasn't special, but I wasn't reserving my first time for any specific person. Sex just didn't seem like the big deal that all the after-school specials made it out to be. My vagina wasn't a flower that wilted with every watering, and my soul wasn't marked for hell or whatever bullshit Amber sometimes talked about. I also didn't feel magically closer to Adam. Technically, we were closer because we had done probably the most physically intimate thing you could do with another person. Still, we couldn't read each other's minds after we started having sex – although I always knew when he wanted sex, which was always. We had a shared experience, but was it any different than Shelly and my shared experience of going to watch 8 mile together without Lisa and Amber?

By the time high school ended, Shelly, Lisa, and even Amber had experienced their first time, and probably half of my graduating class. Adam and I were still dating and vowed to make our relationship work, even though I had been accepted to a small, private art college an hour away. He took a year off to figure out what he wanted to do and played in his band. Even though Shelly and her boyfriend had broken up right after graduation because they knew going to different colleges would be too difficult, and even though I had seen firsthand the number of guys – college guys – at the college, I thought it would be easy for Adam and me. He was great; we were pretty good at sex after all our practice, and I really loved hanging out with him. Being away from my boyfriend for most of the year wasn't all that bad, was it?

# And I'm Only in College

I loved art, but I didn't realize how much at first. I hadn't been exposed to more than the average field trip or coloring books. I loved films and TV. I was fascinated by cameras – film and photography. I took up photographs before I could walk. I loved to create a shared memory that would live forever. I thought the only thing I could do was make Hollywood movies if I went to art school and got into production. The movies I watched growing up informed so much of my career decisions. *The Holiday* made me fall in love with creating movie trailers, which were essentially mini-movies, *But I'm A Cheerleader* showed me how films could carry an important message in an easy-to-swallow fashion. I could be a part of creating mediums that reached people. *Hedwig and the Angry Inch* was the movie that made me want to make movies. It showed me that I could make art, be weird, and be loved for who I was. I wanted to produce films like Hedwig, and to do that, I had to make money, so I decided to pursue advertising that would give me the money I needed to make the movie I wanted to make.

My parents weren't surprised I decided to go to a small, private college instead of a state college. "You were born to stand out from the crowd," my mom told me as I finished packing up the car as soon as I could move into my dorm. I might not have had to worry about getting lost in a sea of students, but my experience in art school was probably no different than at a state college. It just had fewer people. We still had parties just about every night, and there was more than one night in the week that I would spend the evening drawing with a bottle of wine beside me to help with concentration.

"Jess, what are you doing hiding in your room?" my next-door dorm mate demanded. "Come play Slap the Bag with us."

"What's Slap the Bag?" I asked, dropping the colored pencil and abandoning my work.

Kaley linked her arm with mine, dragging me toward the common room on our floor. There were nine double rooms and four single rooms on each floor. The common room hadn't changed since the 80s. Chairs with wooden arms and green cushions were sprawled everywhere. There was a round table that some people studied at, but mostly homed boxes of pizza. One door led outside, and the door opposite our floor entrance led to another set of rooms. "Only the best game ever. Okay, we have this bag of Franceza, right? Whoever is holding it chooses someone to slap it while they drink from the spout. And the person can slap it as many times as they want."

"Is there a winner? Do I lose?"

"No, we get drunk. Come on!"

The alcohol was passed around, and the room became louder and louder as we got drunker. Kaley bumped her arm into mine. "Where's Adam?"

"Probably at home. Why?"

"Why isn't he here?"

Kaley thought he was a student here. "Oh, he doesn't go here. He just comes out to visit me."

"Then he needs to come more often. You're the coolest, Jess, so he is also the coolest."

I thought about Adam. Was he cool? Was I cool? I hadn't really thought about it. I looked around at the people in the room. They were all people I knew because their names were always on other people's lips, and they wanted to hang out and get drunk with me. I guess I was cool. And if Adam was cool because of me, then there was nothing to it.

He was the perfect candidate for a typical college cool guy. He was still in his band. I think part of the reason I stayed with Adam despite our physical distance was that band. I had helped name it HA! – Happy Aliens! when the guys were brainstorming names. They wanted to call themselves something stupid like Ranger or Yellow Dress. Thank God I was able to convince them to go with my suggestion. I didn't stop with band names, though. I was the one who worked on their marketing, logo, and posters. I wasn't just Adam's girlfriend. I was basically another member of the band, just not a musician. If it weren't for me, they would only be playing in their garage. With my help, they were able to separate themselves from the other groups who called themselves bands but never got out of the garage.

Besides Adam, my favorite person in the band was Phoenix. He was a year younger than Adam and myself and a fantastic guitar player. On the weekend, he came out with Adam to visit me. Half the single girls in my dorm and some of the non-single girls always found a way to be around us. It made Adam and I laugh, but it seemed like Phoenix didn't notice the attention he was attracting.

Kaley bumped my arm again. "So when Adam comes up to visit you next, can he bring that other guy too?"

"Phoenix?"

"Oh my god, he is so hot. Does he have a girlfriend? Oh, it doesn't matter." She laughed. "What happens on a college visit stays on a college visit."

I laughed with her, but my insides churned. I didn't want Phoenix hooking up with Kaley. I didn't want him hooking up with anyone.

"Can you give me his number? Or better yet, I'll text him from your phone."

"My battery is dead," I lied quickly. "Tomorrow?" I hoped she would forget we had this conversation tomorrow. Why was I being so possessive? It's not like she wanted to text Adam. Did I have a crush on Phoenix? No. I brushed that thought away. I was with Adam.

The next morning, after I nursed my hangover with coffee and greasy sausages, I thought about Phoenix and Adam. Whenever my mind wandered over to Phoenix, I tried to push Adam's face front and center in my memories. Maybe it was a crush, but there's nothing wrong with a crush. Everyone has crushes. I knew that Adam had a crush on a tall, red-headed server, but it didn't bother me because I knew he wouldn't do anything. Just like I wouldn't do anything with Phoenix.

Later that day, after staring at my art book and flipping through magazines at the desk that lined a wall in my room, unable to focus, I called Adam. Even though I knew the crush I had on Phoenix wasn't a big deal, I still felt a bit guilty. It didn't help that he was stuck back home while I was living the life as a college girl and having an amazing time.

"Hello?" His voice sounded groggier than mine.

"Hey, what's up?"

Adam grunted. "Not much."

"How's practice?"

"S'fine."

We sat in silence. Okay, I know I called him, but why did I have to be the one to carry this conversation.

"I miss you. Kaley was asking about you."

"Oh yeah?"

"Yeah, she said you should come up more often."

"Maybe."

I rolled my eyes. Throw me any kind of bone here, Adam! "Well, you sound busy," I said sarcastically.

"What's that supposed to mean?"

"It means I called to have a conversation, not to just be grunted at."

"I don't know what you want from me," he started to speak louder. I got annoyed.

"I want a conversation."

"About what? What do we have to talk about?"

"Tell me about your day, or something weird, or whatever."

"Nothing happens. I work. I practice. That's it. I'm not an exciting college boy."

"I'm not asking you to be. God. Why is this so hard?" I slapped my pillow with frustration.

"Everything is fine, Jess. I'm just tired, that's all."

I sighed. This was Adam. Things were different now, with me in college. It wasn't like we could spend as much time together as we used to. I could ignore the tension because it was Adam.

The next few weeks passed, and neither of us addressed the tension that arose during that phone call. We talked a little bit less each day, and I tried to tell myself it was okay because I was in class. I had assignments. I loved what I was doing and what I was learning. And I loved hanging out with my new friends. College is a fresh start, not just high school part two. I had to branch out beyond high school. I had to start working out who I would be after college.

On a Friday afternoon in November, I walked into my room and checked my phone. I had left it charging while I took my last class of the day. There were a dozen messages from Adam, all wanting me to call him. I didn't waste time and tapped his photo icon on my phone.

"Hey, Adam, what's up?"

I barely got the words out when he started to rage. "They cut me from the band!"

"What?"

"The assholes, they think they can do this without me. They're wrong. It was all my idea, and without me, they're going to be nothing."

That wasn't completely accurate, but I wasn't about to correct him when he was this upset.

"Why did they kick you out?" I asked.

"Some bullshit reason."

"Okay, what is it?"

"It doesn't matter why, Jess! Okay? They fucking kicked me out like I'm some kind of Yoko or some shit."

While Adam raged in my ear, I considered the reasons HA! might have asked Adam to leave. He was working full-time hours and had just recently started taking courses at a community college. I'm sure they just felt he had too much on his plate, that he couldn't divide his focus any longer.

"Isn't this bullshit?" Adam asked me.

"Of course it is," I said soothingly. "It's absolutely not fair." My phone dinged in my ear with the sound of a text notification. I looked at it, and it was William, the drummer. His text stated he was sure I had heard about Adam but that they'd still love for me to help out if I wanted to. Shortly after William's text came in, I got another one from Damian, the bassist, and the first guy Shelly slept with. He texted the same thing.

"Are you even listening?" Adam accused.

"Of course I am. I'm sorry, I just don't know what to say beyond I'm sorry and it's fucked up."

"Right? Whatever, I'm just going to go for a drive."

"Why don't you try to talk to them?"

"Fuck 'em. If they don't want me, I don't want them," he ended the call without saying goodbye.

There was one band member who I hadn't heard from yet. I found Phoenix's name in my phone's address book and tapped on his picture.

He didn't even say hello when he answered. "I guess you've spoken to Adam."

"You could say that. He's really upset."

"Look, do you have the time to come here? It would be better to talk in person, but I want to assure you that we'll still be friends, and honestly, everything will work out. Some conversations are better in person, though." I was naive enough to think that we actually would stay friends. I wanted to believe it.

I had nothing better to do that night, and I really wanted to sort everything out. I loved HA! and I loved doing the publicity and marketing. It was my first foray into the career that I had always known I wanted for myself, and I didn't want to give it up.

"I can do that. I'll be there in a few hours."

"I'm working; so can you pick me up from work?"

For the one-hour drive from college to my hometown took, I wondered what I would say. I wondered what he would say. I knew that some people would say that I would have to cut these people out of my life to support Adam, but that didn't seem fair! Just because Adam and I shared parts of our lives didn't mean I had to give up relationships with other people, did it? Those relationships meant something to me. I didn't want to throw them away just like that.

The sun was beginning to set as I turned into the parking lot of Phoenix's work, and I saw him standing outside waiting for me. He got in the car before I turned off the engine. "Where should we go?"

"Let's go down by the river." Phoenix put on his seatbelt as I reversed out of the parking spot and back onto the road. He smelled good. He probably put on a cologne after work. No one wanted to smell of their work, even if coffee wasn't a bad smell. "Thanks for coming down."

"It was nice to get out of the dorms anyway," I told him. We didn't speak until I found a semi-secluded spot by the river, surrounded by trees.

It wasn't as cold as past Novembers, even with the sun practically gone, but all the same, I pulled on a warm hat I kept in my car before we walked over to some large rocks to sit. Neither of us seemed to want to talk about the reason I drove down, and we spent a few moments awkwardly talking about school, about work, about everything but Adam.

Finally, he sighed. "Look, it totally sucks about Adam, but you have to know it wasn't something we decided on a whim. He's just so busy, and I get it, but we really want someone to be able to commit 100 percent of the time."

"I know."

"And we definitely still want you to be part of the band. But I understand if you don't want to."

"I don't want to give things up just because Adam can't do something. If I did that, then I wouldn't have gone to college. I love helping you guys. Seeing the posters around town and knowing I made them? That's an amazing feeling."

"Will Adam be mad?"

"He'll be totally pissed. So maybe I won't tell him about it at first. I'll let him cool down a bit first. He'll understand eventually."

"You're super cool, you know that?" Phoenix rubbed his hands together and blew into them to warm them up.

"I have been told by some people that I'm cool." I laughed. "It's getting cold, though, and I still have to drive back."

"Yeah, it's freezing out!"

We jumped up from the rocks and rushed back to the car. I started it to blast the heat and warm us up before we started moving again. The chorus of Fireflies by Owl City was playing on the radio. "I love this song!" I turned the volume up.

"Me too!" Phoenix said.

When the chorus hit, Phoenix began singing along softly in my ear. The hair on the back of my neck prickled when I felt his breath lightly touch my skin. What was happening?

We were both edging closer and closer together and before I even had a chance to think about it, we kissed. I may have kissed other guys than Adam, but I had kissed Adam the most, and I was so used to his lips and his touch so there was something different and exhilarating about kissing Phoenix. It wasn't as if his lips were any different – lips were lips after all, but it felt sweeter, less demanding. Usually, when I kissed Adam, we had sex, unless, of course, he was kissing me good-bye. If I had to give a percentage of how many times our kissing led to sex more recently than not, I'd have to say 90% of the time, one led to the other. This kiss was just a kiss. We weren't fumbling for clothes; we weren't wiggling our tongues in each other's mouths like salmon trying to swim up water. We were just connecting with our lips. We were connecting with more than our lips, but our lips were the conduit for the outpouring of emotion we felt.

I pulled away first, but I didn't say anything. I just reversed the car and silently drove to Phoenix' home. I'm glad it was less than five minutes away. I don't think I'd ever sat in silence for longer than five minutes. There was a part of me that wanted to scream.

"Thanks for the ride," Phoenix said as soon as I parked in his parent's driveway.

"No problem. Thanks for the chat. I'm glad we did that." Oh God, he was going to think I meant the kiss. Well, who cares? I was glad for the kiss too. It was a super sweet kiss.

"Yeah. Okay, talk to you later." He shut the car door, and I watched him run into the house before I reversed out of the driveway. I turned up the radio to fill the car with music and to avoid the thoughts that were now racing to my mind.

I had kissed someone who wasn't Adam. I can't believe I did that. Did that make me a slut? A cheater? I hated that word. I didn't drive to talk to Phoenix with the intention of kissing him. I was forty-five minutes out of town when I realized I hadn't even considered visiting Adam. If he found out that I had driven home and not come by to see him, he would be so hurt.

"He is probably drunk and stoned," I said out loud. That was true, but why didn't it make me feel any better?

The kiss was amazing, though. There were no strings attached, like the expectation to have sex. Not that I minded having sex because I definitely didn't, but sometimes you just want a kiss to be a kiss. Kissing Phoenix made me feel seen for me. Not as a conquest, or a routine, but as a person. I don't know if I'd ever felt that before.

***

Adam was never invited back into the band, and somehow I never spoke to any of them again despite my initial intentions. Adam seemed to get over his anger at being kicked out of the band, but there were some days when he would curse the band and then would be in a foul mood for hours. I couldn't help but notice the distance that seemed to grow between us, but we would still talk about our future.

"Where would we live in New York?" I asked him one Saturday afternoon in January. He had come out to visit for the day but was snowed in until at least the next day. We were lying on my bed, his arm underneath my neck as we cuddled together. I could hear people having conversations outside my room as my dormmates enjoyed their snowy Saturday.

"The Village."

"When are you going to win the lottery, Mr. Money Bags?" I poked him in his belly. "I'm pretty sure it costs a million dollars to rent a box in The Village."

"Okay, what do you think?"

"I think we should go visit and window shop places. That way, we can get a good idea of where to look and what we're looking for. There's a course in school that has us going to the city, so I'm going to take it."

"And then after we move?"

"Then I get a couple of dogs, get an amazing job in a marketing firm, and we party all night."

"Just like that?"

"Just like that." I kissed him and pressed play on my laptop to start the movie we decided on.

Suddenly, it was February, and I was almost finished my first year of college. We had plans to get together for Valentine's Day and combine my birthday celebration, as my birthday was the following week.

I was deciding between a purple flower necklace and a silver chain when the phone rang. I assumed it was Adam telling me he was going to be late to pick me up because the roads were bad. "Hey, you. Are the roads…"

"I don't think this is working," he blurted out, not letting me finish my question.

"What?" Disbelief shaped my words. It wasn't that I couldn't believe he was breaking up with me; it was that he was doing it on Valentine's Day. I had bought him a gift. Could he have done this a few weeks earlier, so I didn't have to waste my money?

"It's just so hard with you being there and me being here. And you're talking about moving to New York."

"We were talking about moving," I said, putting the emphasis on "we."

"That was your thing. It wasn't mine."

"Okay," I said.

"We've grown apart."

"I can't believe you're doing this now. Today."

"I've been thinking about this for a while."

"Then why are you doing this on Valentine's Day?" *And just before my birthday*! I couldn't help but think.

"I just couldn't live a lie anymore."

I scoffed and hung up on him, holding the phone away from my face in shock. I shrieked in frustration, grabbed the present I had bought him – a box set of his favorite horror films, gathered his sweater that he had left behind, ran outside, and tossed it in a snowbank. If he wanted it, then he could drive out here and thaw it out on his own.

I knocked on Kaley's door when I came back inside.

"Hey, girlfriend, what's up?" she asked.

"Adam dumped me," I shouted.

"On Valentine's Day?"

I nodded.

"Well fuck him. You don't need him."

I repeated that phrase in my mind for several days when the hurt and the anger warred with each other. I didn't need him. I was young. I was in college. I was surrounded by available men. I didn't need Adam. I didn't need anyone.

***

Jacob approached me on the quad one day in March. It was a small school, and word had traveled that I was single, probably thanks to Kaley. I kept the guys at arm's length while I dealt with the emotional aftermath of the breakup. I wasn't going to cloister myself like a nun, but I needed a minute. Guys like Jacob seemed content with biding their time. But it was three weeks. I was done licking my wounds. Adam who? "Hey, have plans tonight?" he asked, walking in step with me.

I shrugged. "I'll see what's going on before I decide." In the past, I would have blown him off entirely. I'd tell him I was doing homework, hanging with girlfriends, or something. Something had changed. I knew it, and I knew he could tell.

Jacob smiled. "Maybe I'll come by and see you tonight."

Jacob was cute. He was a typical country boy. Tall, broad shoulders with sandy blond hair. He never got angry that I blew him off. We'd have lunch together sometimes, and we'd laugh and joke. He never mentioned Adam or me being single. It was casual. I think I liked casual.

"Maybe you should," I said.

Before Jacob stopped by, I cleaned my room. I hid the chocolate bar wrappers and condom boxes. I did my best to smooth the lumps from my bed, although I'm not sure if it mattered. Maybe lumps would make tonight more fun.

Jacob was the second guy I had sex with. After months of sex with Adam, I wasn't sure what to expect. Did Adam and I do it differently than other people? Of course, the basics were all the same. The penis goes into the vagina.

The best thing about Jacob was that he didn't expect anything from me. I had just ended a relationship; I wasn't looking for a new one. I wanted fun, and fun I had.

Of course, statistically speaking, I was bound to find a few duds; I just wasn't expecting to find a dud so soon off the bat.

I had met Ezra in Workshop 101. He had blond hair, blue eyes, and this air of innocence around him. He was one of the boys Kaley and I talked about.

"I swear to God he was homeschooled," Kaley mentioned almost every single time.

"No, he's not weird enough," I said.

"But he is weird."

"Kaley, we're in art school. Everyone is fucking weird."

She chugged back her beer and placed the empty bottle on the desk I was sitting at. "Whatever."

I was still finishing my beer, and I put my feet up on her bed. "So what if I told you he invited me to his room tonight."

Kaley's mouth dropped. "What did you say?"

"I said yes."

"Jess! Oh my God!"

"What?" I asked. "Maybe he's really good in bed. I'll treat it like an experiment."

"You have to tell me everything."

"Obviously!"

Kaley jumped off the bed and pushed my feet off. "So what are you going to wear?"

When I knocked on Ezra's door, I could hear Creep playing on his stereo. He invited me in, and we both sat on his bed, listening to more Radiohead. Despite his shyness, he was cute. He looked at me, and I leaned forward and kissed him. I knew he didn't just invite me over to listen to music.

We pivoted so we were facing each other, and our necks didn't get kinked from our awkward position. His hands clutched my sides, and I opened my mouth and welcomed in his tongue. Not a bad kisser. Not the best, but not terrible.

I moved my hands down from around his shoulders to the bottom of his shirt. Grabbing the hem, I tried to lift his shirt over his head, but he pulled back. "Let's just cuddle."

I paused for a moment. Cuddle? "O… Kay." He leaned back against the wall, so I did the same. Was he trying to prolong the moment? Was he worried he'd blow too soon?

I looked around the room for the first time since I got there, and I suddenly understood. There was a poster of a Christian band on his wall, and he had hung a WWJD bracelet from the corner hook. Ezra wasn't going to have sex with me tonight. He wasn't going to have sex until marriage. What was I doing there?

After a quiet moment that seemed like hours, Ezra put his arms around my shoulder and began to kiss me. I kissed him back, but it was very mechanical at that point. I was too young to go through the motions. He kissed my cheek, then my ear, then blew on my neck. I know he thought it would turn me on, but it was pathetic. What did he have to offer me? A relationship with barely any physical intimacy? A church wedding when we graduated? Kids? A white picket fence?

"Ezra, I have to go."

"What?" he murmured into my neck. "Why?"

"My dog ate my homework."

"We can't have dogs in dorms." He laughed and tried to nibble my earlobe.

"Oh, God." I groaned, grossed out. "I, uh, just remembered I have homework to do." I got off the bed as fast as I could, away from him.

"It's Friday." He knew I was giving him an excuse, but I didn't care.

"It's a lot of homework. I don't want to get behind." My earlobe still felt wet, and I rubbed it to remove any trace of him. He didn't move, other than to put a pillow over his lap. I rolled my eyes and left his room without another word. He obviously wanted sex; why didn't he act on it – I was right there!

I didn't even bother knocking on Kaley's door. "What a waste of a Friday night!" I slumped into her desk chair and took a swig of the can of beer she handed to me.

"I told you he was weird!"

"Weird doesn't even cover it. Oh my God. What if other people knew I was spending time with him? What if they think I'm," I gulped dramatically, "celibate?"

Kaley laughed, then started to cough when the bubbles from her beer got in the way of her laugh. "You're such a drama queen. No one thinks that. Hello? Adam, Jacob."

"People like Ezra need to have a sign or something. Then I wouldn't waste my time or theirs. Though I care more about my time, obviously."

"Obviously." Kaley was uncharacteristically silent for a minute. Something was up; I knew it. "What about Leo?"

"Excuse me, Leo?" Leo, one of the hottest guys in college, if not the hottest? Leo, one of the most talented guys in college? Leo with the sexy voice? Leo with the girlfriend?

"You literally just shut down. So yah, Leo."

Leo had been the talk of Kaley and me for months. Even when I was with Adam, even when I was sleeping with Jacob, I couldn't help but notice Leo. He was tall. He filled a pair of jeans and a pull-over long-sleeve shirt like no one else could. "Leo has a girlfriend."

"I don't think he does. Haven't you heard the rumors?"

"There are rumors?"

"Girl. He has been going to parties solo. Who does that if they have a girlfriend."

"Oh, my God." I breathed. I bet Leo was an amazing kisser. I bet he was amazing at sex. "Wait, it's not like I have a chance with him."

"Why not?" Kaley stood up. "Okay, so there's a party in the west dorms. I bet he's there. It's still early, so let's go."

"And what if he's there?"

"Then you talk to him, dipshit!"

I looked down at what I was wearing. It was okay for Ezra, but Leo needed more. I wanted him to see me look amazing. "I have to change."

After the fastest change ever, with Kaley breathing down my neck, we made our way toward the party. We heard it before we saw it, and we quickly got caught up in the reverie. I watched Kaley join a round of Slap the Bag while I drank a strongly poured vodka and soda. I glanced around the room, looking for Leo without making it look like I was looking for Leo.

I heard Kaley clear her throat loudly and looked at her. Her eyes bulged out of her face and then looked pointedly next to me. I turned my head and almost dropped my drink. How long had Leo been beside me?

"Oh hey," Leo said when he saw me. "You're Jess, right? We haven't met officially, but I've seen you around a lot."

*Don't fuck this up, don't fuck this up*, I repeated. I hoped to God my face didn't reflect my almost panicked mantra as I smiled at him and tapped his red solo cup with mine.

We stood there, shoulders almost touching, while the music played. In a brief moment of silence between songs on the playlist, I took my opportunity. "This is a pretty decent party," I said.

He smiled at me. Leo smiled at me. I smiled back. Was I showing too much teeth? Too little? It was as if I had never talked to a guy before. You are a strong, independent woman, Jessi! You don't need his approval. But it was Leo. You don't need a man's approval to sleep with him. Think about how good it would feel. I mentally shook off my awkwardness as much as I could and tossed a patented Jess smile. It always worked on Adam. It had worked on Jacob. It sorts of worked on Ezra, even if he didn't do anything about it.

"Wanna get out of here?" Leo asked me, his lips just barely grazing my ear. I shivered.

"Yah, I do."

I caught Kaley's eye and gestured that I was leaving with him. She gestured back that she was fine to stay where she was. God, I loved her. Best wingman ever.

Leo's dorm was a bit further from the party than mine was, and every step made the anticipation sweeter. In romantic comedies, most times the sex came out of nowhere. There was a spontaneous look between the two leads, and then they'd be in each other's arms. Real life wasn't like that. Real life was acknowledging that you wanted to have sex with the other person and you went to a location where you could have sex.

As soon as the door was shut, Leo turned on some music. Obviously, he was expecting me to be loud because he wasn't shy about the volume. When he kissed me, I wrapped my arms around his neck and met his energy with my own. This definitely was not a waste of a Friday night.

I was happy he turned the music up because he was not afraid to push every single one of my buttons, and I was not afraid to tell him how much I enjoyed it. He came so hard, it almost made me want to start all over again.

Leo held me against him as he spooned me, and we worked to catch our breath. "So that was fun," he said.

"It really was," I said.

"You can stay over if you want."

I was glad I wasn't facing him. I didn't want to look too eager, but holy shit! Was this not a one-night stand? I was totally fine with it being a one-night stand. Was this going to turn into something more?

"I am pretty comfortable." I pushed my butt closer to his crotch.

"You do that again; I'll have to do something about it."

"Is that a challenge?"

I had multiple texts on my phone the next day from Kaley. I typed out a quick message that I was alright and that I would tell her everything but that Leo and I were going to have breakfast. She sent me multiple emojis detailing her excitement, and I put my phone back in my pocket.

Leo and I were having breakfast. In public. Leo held my hand as we walked to breakfast. In public. That's not something you did with a one-night stand. This was pre-relationship behavior. It was practically a relationship. I was practically in a relationship with the hottest guy in college!

After that first breakfast, he came back to my dorm, and we hung out with Kaley. That Sunday, we went for lunch off campus. Then Monday, I went to his dorm after class and stayed the night. Tuesday, he came back to my dorm and spent the night.

"You guys are totally dating!" Kaley said the following Monday, a rare night that I wasn't sleeping at Leo's and he wasn't staying at mine.

"Right? How did this happen?" I said.

Kaley raised her hand. "I'd like to thank the Academy for this award."

I laughed. "This is just perfect. Out with the old, in with the extremely hot."

Three weeks after we started dating, something didn't seem right. It was a small college, and it wasn't uncommon to see the same people over and over again as we all walked to our respective classes, but I couldn't remember the last time I had seen Leo.

That night, there was a knock on my door. I opened it, and Leo stood outside. "Hey, beautiful." He greeted me and walked into my room.

"Hey! I didn't see you today."

He helped me pull off my sweater. "I was around."

"I mean, so was I."

Instead of responding, Leo kissed me, and then we were both naked, and then he was lying on top of me, and then I forgot that I hadn't seen him that day.

But I didn't see him the day after that either. Leo had told me that he couldn't stay the night, which was fine with me. I made an effort to be extra observant as I walked to classes and grabbed food, but it was like he didn't exist in the daytime anymore. Around 8:00 that night, I got a text from him asking if I'd come see him that night. I sent him a text in response saying, that I had some work to do, but would I see him at lunch the next day? He didn't respond.

I sat at our usual table in the cafeteria the next day, hoping that he would show up. He didn't. I expected a knock on the door that night, but the only person who came by was the Resident Advisor, reminding me and everyone else on the floor to clean out the lint traps in the dryer.

"Kaley, have you seen Leo around?" I asked her that Friday.

She shook her head. "I actually haven't. Have you texted him?"

"No, I've reached the quota of texts that are appropriate to send without sounding clingy." Besides, I didn't want to need him. I was empowered. I was in charge of my own sexuality. But why wasn't he texting me back, and why was he avoiding me?

Two more days after I sent my last text and made myself promise not to send any more until I had heard from him, I walked into a common area after my last class of the day. Leo! Leo was there. In the common room. With a – who the fuck was the girl with him? Calm down, Jess. It could be a friend. Or a cousin. Or a goddamn girlfriend, that motherfucker! My attempts to be logical in the face of the puzzle failed, and I stormed out of the common area the way I came in. I went through every single conversation we had with each other in my head. Then I thought about everything he didn't say.

I made it to my room, and I slammed my books down on the desk. He had never said he wanted me to be his girlfriend. I just assumed that I was. I stood in front of the mirror. *"You have to forget about him,"* I told my reflection. Forgetting guys was easy. I never thought about Adam, or Phoenix, or Ezra.

I rummaged in my drawer beside my bed and pulled out a condom. I held it up ceremoniously. "Goodbye, Leo, you manwhore!" I flung the condom in the trash and took the bin outside the building to dump the contents.

The next morning, I woke up and didn't think about Leo at all. Ha! I win. *You have no power over me, you hot piece of dick. I didn't care that I didn't see Leo all day.* I laughed with Kaley and made plans for our next weekend party.

The next morning, while I was still waking up, my phone chimed with a text notification. I frantically reached out to grab my phone, only to be disappointed to see it was a text from my mother and not from Leo.

I remembered when I was still in high school, with my friends reading Cosmo on my bed. "Pisces are incorrigible romantics. In their search for love, they tend to forget about their moral values sometimes." Shelly had read off to me.

"What does 'incorrigible' mean?" I had asked.

Shelly had shrugged. "I don't know."

"Fucking Pisces," I groaned in my college dorm bed while my mom's text asking about when I was next coming home was left unanswered.

I ran into Dave one morning a week after I had thrown out the ceremonial condom. "You okay?" he asked when I didn't return his exuberant greeting.

I sighed. "I'm fine. Just…"

"Leo?" he finished.

"No. Not Leo. I'm not thinking about Leo; I'm not talking about Leo."

"Okay, but you've said his name like three times."

"Shut up, Dave." I saw his tray of breakfast food. "Sit with you?"

"Yah, come on."

Dave had been at a party that Kaley and I had attended, and we became fast friends. He laughed with us about Ezra, and he empathized with me about Leo. It was nice to have a friend who didn't have ulterior motives. With Leo out of the picture, though, Dave and I started spending more time together. I realized I had started looking for him in the cafeteria and walking around the quad. I texted him if I hadn't seen him that day if he hadn't texted me first.

We were watching a movie on his laptop, and I was resting my head on his shoulder. "I think we should date," he told me.

"I think we should, too."

When I told Kaley, she rolled her eyes. "Took you guys long enough."

"Oh, come on, it wasn't that bad."

"Whatever," Kaley said. "Now you have to find out once and for all why he always has money. Like, is he rich?"

"I can't just ask someone if they're rich."

"Yes, you can! Especially if you're fucking. I'm assuming you're fucking."

"Obviously. But I still can't ask him."

"Come on. He always drops more money than you do, and he doesn't even have a job. Maybe he's a prostitute."

"He's not a prostitute, Kaley! I think I'd know."

Kaley's phone started to ring. "Oh, it's Jay. Gotta run, but find out what he does. I'm dying to know!"

I couldn't stop thinking about Dave's job. If he even had a job. I was mad at Kaley for making me care about it so much. Why should I care? It didn't affect me. But she was right. He didn't work, but he was always paying for things. It just didn't make sense. Finally, I thought of the most ridiculous thing I could think of and asked him. It was so ridiculous that he'd laugh and then naturally tell me what he did. It was the perfect solution.

"Dave, do you sell drugs?" I asked.

He looked at me. "Don't get mad."

Oh my God. He does sell drugs! "I'm not mad."

The silence stretched between us. Was he going to say something? Was I supposed to follow up on my not being mad? What was happening? "But are you?"

He shrugged. "It's no big deal."

My mind whirled, and I worked to keep a neutral look on my face. He said it wasn't a big deal, so maybe it wasn't. Maybe it was just weed. Weed wasn't drugs, not really. It's not like it was meth, or… What if he sold meth? What if he sold really shitty meth and caused a lot of people to pick out their skin and watch their teeth fall out and – Okay, Jess. Calm down. It's no big deal. And it's Dave. You know Dave. You know he wouldn't do anything to hurt you, so there's no way he'd do anything to hurt anyone else. Maybe his meth is the good meth that doesn't cause teeth to fall out or people to pick at their skin. If it wasn't him, then it would probably be some gangster who would kill a person if they didn't use as many drugs as he wanted.

The semester ended, and Kaley and I decided to live off dorms for the next semester. We had found the perfect apartment for the two of us. Living off dorms was as good as I had hoped. We were no longer the babies on campus and we had even more freedom than ever.

"This is such a great space," Dave told me one evening. "I could see myself living in a place like this. With an actual job."

"There's an apartment that's available for rent on the first floor," I told him. Kaley and I lived on the top floor. I always told people we were on the top floor, even though there were only three floors. It seemed more metropolitan to say "the top floor."

"Maybe I should take a look," he said.

That night after he left, I lay in my bed and once again thought about his job selling drugs. It never came between us, and I knew he didn't take what he sold. He was just so amazing. He listened when I talked; he never rushed me or gave any indication that he was bored or annoyed by what I was saying. The sex was amazing, and even if his job wasn't the most traditional, at least he was making money.

A month later, I was helping him move into the unit on the first floor. "This is going to be amazing," I told him after I dropped a pile of blankets on his unmade bed. "I can help you find a job too."

"Yeah," he said noncommittally. "Sounds good."

When I went back to my apartment after helping Dave unpack some more, Marcus was in the living room playing video games with Kaley. "Oh, hey Marcus," I called out. "What's new?"

"Not a thing. Except kicking Kaley's ass."

"It's because you cheat!" Kaley said. "Did you get all of Dave's things?"

I sat in a floral-printed oversized chair. "All moved in. He's just got to organize."

"You're brave," Marcus said.

"What do you mean?" I asked him.

"You're practically living with him."

I laughed. "Barely. He's like two floors down."

"Jess and Dave, playing house." He set down his game controller triumphantly. "And that's another one."

"I swear to God. you're cheating!" Kaley said. "Again."

"Hey, I'm having a party next month. You guys are coming, right?" He looked at me. "And bring your husband."

I threw a small cushion at his head on my way to the kitchen.

Marcus was wrong. It wasn't like we were living together. We were together a lot, but we always had our own space. It was nice to have Dave so close by, though.

Late one night, there was a knock on my door. Kaley wasn't home, so I left my bedroom to see who was there, though I was almost positive it would be Dave.

"Hey, what's up?" I asked.

"Come with me." He took my hand and led me to the stairwell, but instead of going downstairs, we went up.

"I thought this door was locked." I had seen people on the roof of my building, but I hadn't yet figured out how to get up there. Every time I thought of exploring, I was already doing something else.

"It's never locked."

Even though the building had only three floors, we were in an area of the city that didn't have a lot of high rises, so we were still able to enjoy the view without concrete buildings in the way.

"It's great up here. I can breathe and not worry about anything," he told me.

"What do you have to worry about?" I asked, wrapping my arms around his waist tightly.

He kissed my forehead. "Nothing." It was warm out, so despite the lateness and the rain that had started to fall, neither of us made any effort to leave.

He kissed me deeply, and his hands rose to my shoulders and squeezed them. Then they fell to my shirt hem. He pulled off my t-shirt and tossed it beside us, and pulled off his own shirt. Then, the two of us took off our pants and we lay down on the pile of discarded clothes.

As he moved inside me, I was struck by the different kinds of sex someone could experience. The first time Dave and I had sex, it was a mad dash of getting naked and feeling every part of our bodies. We've also had rushed sex, the most recent in the closet before Kaley came home, just to say we did it, and then that night, we had slow sex, the kind they call making love.

There we were, on the roof, under the stars, exposed to nature. It was amazing; the stars in the sky matched the stars in my eyes, but it didn't last. It was only a few days later that I learned he had started to use the same drugs he was selling.

The night of Marcus's party, Dave and I had a fight before we even got to the party. Our fights were becoming more frequent. I would get upset that he was unreachable for hours or even a day at a time. He would get upset that I was spending time with other people who weren't him. Sometimes we'd even fight because I wanted to get Chinese food and he wanted pizza.

The two of us tried to hide any emotional evidence of the fight when we got to the party. I quickly drank the first drink that was given to me – a disgusting, warm beer – and I went to find something better.

"You're drinking too much," he said snarkily.

I whirled around to face him. "Excuse me?" I didn't let him finish. "I had one beer that was practically water, and who are you, my liver? I'll drink what I want to drink."

I had raised my voice by the end of my sentence, and the people closest to us were starting to pay attention.

"I'm just saying you'll feel like shit tomorrow."

"Then I'll feel like shit. It's my decision." I poured half a cup of rum and added soda to it.

"Fucking Jess, I'm not going to hold your hair back for you."

"I'm not asking you to." I took a gulp of my drink, knowing that I had made it too strong to prove a point but not wanting him to see it. I tried to push myself past him, but he grabbed my upper arm. I shook off his hand and tried to create more distance between the two of us, but he grabbed me again, harder and with both hands.

"What the fuck, get your hands off me!" I shouted. Two guys I didn't know surged forward and pulled Dave away from me. "Fuck off!" I shouted and left the apartment.

I held my cup in my teeth as I quickly sent a text to Marcus, telling him why I had left, apologizing, and saying I'd see him later. I had finished drinking by the time I got back to my building, and since Kaley wasn't home yet, I changed into my pajamas and fell into bed.

I don't know what woke me up a few hours later, but I knew something wasn't right. I opened my eyes and saw Dave standing over me.

"Jess, I'm sorry; I didn't mean to." Although I couldn't fully see his face, I could tell he was crying. "Please take me back, please." When he reached toward me, I screamed.

"No, shh, it's okay. I'm not going to hurt you," he repeated over and over as I jumped out of the other side of the bed, wanting to be as far from him as possible.

The light in my room flicked on, and I saw Kaley in the doorway, holding a baseball bat. "Get the fuck out of here!" she screeched.

"No, I want to talk to Jess." His body was turned toward Kaley with his hands in the air, but he was looking at me.

"I don't want to talk to you," I said, shivering with fear.

"She doesn't want to talk to you!" Kaley repeated with more authority than I was able to muster.

Convinced by the baseball bat that Kaley refused to put down, Dave eventually left. He made it difficult to avoid him because he still lived two floors down, but Kaley, Marcus, and I had a system. Between the two of them, I was never leaving my apartment myself. I blocked his number from my phone, and I was extra vigilant at school to make sure I didn't run into him.

After the first week of leaving rooms quickly if I saw him and sandwiching myself between friends if I couldn't leave the room, I started seeing him less.

"I saw him tweaking behind the building," Kaley told me when I mentioned to her that I hadn't seen him in quite some time. "I don't think he's even going to classes anymore. I'm pretty sure they're going to kick him out. He's spending all his money on drugs now."

"I don't know how I'm supposed to feel about that," I told her. "Like, on one hand, it's great I don't have to deal with his bullshit, but on the other hand, it's not like I enjoy seeing him throw his life away."

"You're a far better person than I am," Kaley told me. "I say he deserves what he gets. No one forced him to do this. He did it all on his own."

"Do you think I should have seen the signs sooner?"

Kaley snorted. "No one knew until it got dramatic, so it's not your fault. Don't give him this much air time. He's not worth it."

Maybe Kaley was right, but it didn't help. I felt almost dirty like I had a responsibility to make sure he didn't throw his life away like he had. When I found out he had been kicked out of the apartment, I didn't sleep for two days. I tossed and turned, burdened by guilt for not helping him and guilt for feeling relieved I wouldn't have to deal with him anymore.

I was at another party of Marcus's when I felt I was finally over the guilt of my relationship with Dave. I looked at Marcy's and knew exactly what I needed: a rebound.

Marcus was talking with a buddy of his that I didn't know when I caught his eye and smiled. I had practiced my smile, and I knew it conveyed exactly what I wanted it to convey. Marcus nodded, and I knew I would get my rebound.

He didn't wait for his guests to leave but nodded in the direction of the room furthest from the center of the party. "You're okay with this?" he asked as we took our clothes off.

"So okay." He lay back on the bed and helped me straddle him. "And you know this doesn't mean…"

"Yah, I know," he said. I leaned down and kissed him and let my breasts brush against his chest. He wrapped his arms around my back. "It's good as it is."

I told myself it was fine, and it was fine. I told myself that it didn't bother me that things ended so poorly with Dave. I laughed with my friends as I recounted the stories of life with him, and soon it became a caricature of real life. The thing that I worked really hard to ignore was that in Dave becoming a caricature, I did, too.

I don't think this was the first time I started wrapping myself in a veil of protection; I think I had been doing it all my life. With my girlfriends, they looked to me for answers to the questions their parents wouldn't give them. I couldn't give off the aura of uncertainty like they did. I wanted them to look at me in awe. I wanted them to see I wasn't hurt by the breakups, by the fuckups. The problem was, the path I was going down meant I was hiding myself from me, too.

I didn't know then that the more I hid myself, the harder it would be to find myself later.

# And I'm Only 22

I graduated college and moved to New York City with just a few bags and boxes of stuff in my car. My great-grandmother worked for a Long Island church for forty years, so after her husband died, she sold the house she had lived in with him and moved onto the church property. She was the first person I lived within the city. My first roomie, and a great cook too!

Outside my bedroom window, I could see the bell that chimed daily and woke me up. The front door of our house opened up to the church parking lot.

Prior to moving in with my great-grandmother, I landed an internship at an agency. And after that agency, I found another one.

My first agency was an internship. I was too scared to even apply until a senior in college – Mark convinced me to try it out. "What do you have to lose?" he said. "The worst they can say is no, and then you're in no worse shape than you are right now."

So I applied. As luck would have it, the person who read the applications grew up in Minnesota and actually knew how elite my college was. He snagged me, and I packed the car, but not before thanking Mark.

I learned a lot at that internship: how to run a project, how to help creatives when they're in a rut. I even organized an internship project to help future interns. I went on set, I helped launch a social media campaign for Sour Patch Kids – I was so dedicated I actually shaved SPK into the side of my head.

I also learned what happens when an agency loses a big client: layoffs. My internship was ending, and I was hoping to get a full-time job there, but then the layoffs happened. No one was safe. The guy who hired me was even let go. It was a big layoff for them, and unfortunately, it wasn't going to be a good look to hire the interns that year, even though we were going to be the lowest paid in the agency.

Thankfully, one of my first friends, whom I met at my first agency, Leah, took me under her wing and arranged for me to get a job with her partner at his boutique agency. It was all digital-based and though I had only a bit of experience in digital and web marketing, I took the challenge head-on.

There were three of us at first: the owner, a lovely man from Armenia, and a designer. I had to figure out how to budget projects, make timelines, bring in new clients, and everything in between. It was tough, but I was eager, underpaid but eager.

Despite all the teachings I learned in college, there were certain things I didn't learn until I was on the job.

I learned how to bring in clients. I learned how to run budgets. I also learned that despite all the good things you could bring to a company, they'd still rather pocket that extra money than pay their staff what they're worth. The owner of the umbrella company the small, boutique agencies operated under was notorious for undervaluing her people.

After a year, I gathered up my courage and had a sit-down meeting with Brandi.

"What's up, Jess?" Brandi asked in her posh English accent. Her nails were perfect; her outfit was perfect. She just oozed style and money.

"I've been here a year, Brandi. Actually, my one-year was last month." Brandi nodded but said nothing. "I've been instrumental in bringing in some long-term contracts, and I've taken on the responsibility of running the budgets. I'd like to discuss a raise."

There, I had said it. And my voice stayed strong. I was proud of myself.

Brandi pursed her lips. "I'm sorry, Jess, we just don't have the budget right now."

I wanted to protest. I knew exactly how much money the agency was bringing in, and a lot of that was because of the work I was doing. I didn't protest, though, because what would that have done? Brandi wasn't going to change her mind.

A raise would have been nice, as I had moved out with my grandma already and lived in Bed-Stuy. By the end of the month, I was so broke from being underpaid that I ate ramen and snuck my own PBR to the bar.

The day after I asked Brandi for a raise, I was finishing up a call with a client when I saw her walk in. She knew how to make an entrance, but today she made a spectacle. She was wearing a new fur coat that fell to her knees, with matching boots and a hat. I barely had words to end the call with my client. I knew then that the agency had the budget to give me a raise, but Brandi had preferred to get a new outfit instead.

Not long after, I had a meeting with a potential client. At the meeting, the drinks that were pouring hit me a little too hard. This client took the opportunity to try to take advantage of me. I had viewed this as a potential client meeting, but he obviously was viewing this as a date.

Don was older than me, which wasn't difficult; I was barely out of college in a field full of middle-aged men. He wasn't unattractive, but I wasn't looking for a fling with him. I wanted to sign him to the agency. I wanted his business.

I began the dance of being polite, but not too polite that he would misread my intentions. Unfortunately, he was dancing a different dance. He would stand close to me and try to feed me food. I opened my mouth, knowing this wasn't proper behavior from a client but still wanting to come across as a professional who wanted his business. He moved quickly, sliding down the booth, his head coming close to mine, his own mouth opening, and his tongue darting out, seeking a place in my mouth.

I jerked my head back. "Stop," I told him. "I'm eating."

Don looked at me for a moment, then slid back to a more respectable distance.

The server approached. "What else are you looking for?"

"Let's get some more wine," Don said, his hand slipping under the table and grabbing my thigh.

I shifted my leg away from him. The server left and returned with more wine. Don drank liberally, but I switched to water. I needed all my wits about me with him.

While Don got more drunk, I was sobering up. While an hour ago, I may have tried to still spin this, I knew there was no way he was going to sign with me. I also knew he had no intention of signing with me.

I stood up. "It's been great," I lied.

Don also stood up, but he swayed a little under the influence of the wine. He put his hand around my waist and tried to line up our lips. His final attempt at a kiss failed when I easily stepped away from his grasp. He teetered but caught himself on the table. I gathered my coat and my purse, but before I left, I looked him in his drunken eyes. "You're an asshole for letting me think you wanted to do business." If he had a response to that, I didn't want to hear it, and I left the restaurant. I didn't even take a moment to go pee, though I was desperate. I got off the train, and for the duration of my 15-minute walk, I called a friend to distract me so I didn't have to sneak between cars. I walked as briskly as I could while pinching the best I could at the same time. Only when I was home and safe from an embarrassing accident could I unpack what had happened that evening. I might not have signed him up as a client, but I was proud of myself for standing up to Don.

Don wouldn't be the first man in advertising to think he'd be able to get what he wanted from me. I knew being a woman in advertising in New York City would be difficult, but I thought, maybe foolishly, that it would be different for me. I thought I'd give off a vibe they'd recognize that I wasn't someone who could be messed with. Instead, they saw it as a challenge, someone to be triumphant over. For a long time, I knew I couldn't trust any connection I made with advertising. Did they want to work with me, or did they want to fuck me?

One Friday, after a long day at work – the end of which consisted of me drinking a couple of glasses of red wine, I sat on the train, my exhaustion warring with the giddy feeling of being wine-drunk. I had forty minutes on the train, but my body needed sleep now.

I woke up to someone tapping me on my shoulder. "Hey," I heard. "I think this is your stop." I opened my eyes and saw the person speaking to me. A young black man was standing over me, but when he saw my eyes open, he sat back on the bench beside another black man the same age.

"How did you know?" I asked, standing up.

"White people don't go past this stop," he told me.

I smiled in thanks and left the train. As I walked past the window, I looked in and noticed the shirts the two of them were wearing. They were part of the New York Guardian Angels, a community-run organization that worked to minimize crime in New York neighborhoods.

The next morning, more hungover than I'd like thanks to the wine I had drunk at the office, I went to the convenience store around the corner for a pick-me-up. I found Gatorade and Top Ramen and went to the till to pay.

The woman in line in front of me was arguing with the cashier about her being a dollar short.

"It's one goddamned dollar! I need it for my kid. Are you going to refuse food for my kid over one dollar?" The cashier tried to interrupt, but he was no match for this woman. He wasn't giving up, though, and the woman was getting louder and louder. My head was going to explode if this situation didn't resolve.

I stepped forward and put my purchases on the counter with hers. "I've got it," I said. The cashier didn't hesitate, ringing the items through and moving to the next person.

The woman followed me out of the store. "Thanks for that."

"No problem."

"I don't recognize you," she said. "How long have you lived here?"

"About six months or so."

"Wow!"

"What do you mean?"

"Most white people don't last that long here," she said.

"Why?"

"You know."

I suppose I did know. White people were the minority in that area of New York. Her eyes moved over my face.

"You're in rough shape," she said. "What bar were you at?"

I told her I had come home late from work.

"Alone?"

"Yeah."

"The hell you did! I am the boss lady of this block. I'll keep an eye on you, and I'll tell my boys to do the same. If they see you around, I'll get them to ask who you are. What's your name?"

"Jess."

I won't tell them that," she said. "I'll tell them you're Jazzy J. You tell them who you are, and they'll drop whatever they're doing, and they'll walk you home."

"How will they know to ask me?" I said.

She just laughed. "Oh, honey. You stick out like a sore thumb."

I felt safe in my neighborhood, especially after meeting that block mama, Precious, who pushed her baby around in a Louis Vuitton stroller. Even before I met her, though, I was checking out different bars and pubs and meeting new people. I met Shawn on one of my exploratory nights.

In Minnesota – especially the small town I lived in, there weren't a lot of mixed-race couples. I even had some friends whose parents wouldn't be happy if they started dating someone who wasn't white. Thank God, my parents were far more open-minded. I wasn't taught to judge by color, sex, looks, or anything other than how the person acts inside and out.

When I saw Shawn that night on the opposite end of the bar from me, I knew I wanted to embrace him. He was beautiful. He had close-cut black hair, and that night, I could tell he had just come from the barber because the lines were tight. He wore plain jeans and a long-sleeved shirt, but there was something about the way that he held himself that made it impossible for me to look away.

I picked up my beer and moved to the empty chair beside him. "Hi, I'm Jess." I had learned to just be up front. People will either want to talk or they won't.

"Shawn." We shook hands. This was a good sign.

"What do you do, Shawn?"

"I'm in finance." I swear to God, half the men I met said that, and only an eighth of them were telling the truth. I let it slide, though.

"I'm in advertising."

"So what, you're like Mad Men?" He smiled. Oh my god, his smile. If I had seen that earlier, I would have sat beside him even sooner.

"Yeah, it's exactly like that." I laughed. "You have an amazing smile. Do you get that a lot?"

"I don't hear it enough from beautiful girls like you." He smiled again. He knew what he was doing, and it was working. I leaned my shoulder into him. He was warm, and his warmth spread all over my body.

Before we knew it, the bar was closing, and we were forced to leave. "Why don't you come over to mine?" I asked, interlacing my fingers with his.

"Now? It's late." He was letting me drag him along the sidewalk despite his lackluster protests.

"Or it's early." The bar closed at 4 a.m. Both our arguments were sound.

"Alright, I'll cook for you."

At my apartment, I opened all the cupboard doors so he knew where all our pots and pans were. Despite it being so late and early at the same time, we weren't trying to be quiet. I had just dropped an egg on the floor when Stella, one of my roommates, stumbled from her room.

"For fuck's sake, it's 4:30!" she whispered angrily.

"Sorry, go back to bed," I said, putting the broken eggshells in the garbage.

Stella swore under her breath again but returned to her room. I washed the egg yolk from my hands and looked at Shawn. The two of us laughed while trying not to make a sound, which only made us laugh harder.

"Okay, maybe cooking for me was a bad idea," I said. "But I have something else we can do."

Shawn had the presence of mind to make sure we weren't leaving any burners on, and then he let me lead him to my room. "Can you be quiet?" I asked.

"Depends on what you're going to do to me."

I tugged on the bottom of his shirt. "What do you want me to do?"

We went through the motions of people having sex for the first time: he took off his shirt, then I took off my shirt, but I left my bra on. He touched my breasts and squeezed them a little. Then I reached around and unhooked my bra. His hands felt warm on my breasts when he fondled them.

Then he took off his pants. The bulge I saw there was bigger than anything I had ever seen before. I had always thought it was an urban legend about size. Maybe it still is, but that night, I understood size queens.

For the next two weeks, it was the Jess and Shawn show. Even though neither of us had committed to one another, we were always together. The sex continued to be amazing, and he made me laugh.

Then we drifted apart. There was no huge fight or anything. It was New York, and I was experiencing everything for the first time. I wasn't ready to settle down with anyone – despite the size of his penis, and Shawn said he wasn't either.

A few months after Shawn and I last saw each other, I ran into him at an outdoor summer concert. He wasn't alone, but I didn't think anything of the girl standing beside him. I wasn't alone either – I was with someone I met through Shawn.

What piqued my interest was his expression as he looked between me and the other girl. What was going on?

I decided to play it cool. Most people will hang themselves if you give them enough rope.

"Hi Shawn, it's been a while. How are you?"

"I'm good," he mumbled.

"So of course you know Darius."

"Yeah. Hey man. This is Ashley."

Dammit, he wasn't giving me any information, the sneak.

"Hey Ashley, nice to meet you. I'm Jess."

Ashley smiled warmly. She seemed nice. Fine, I was just going to ask.

"So how long have you two been dating?"

She wrapped her arms around Shawn's waist. She was so petite, her head only reached his shoulders. "It was a year last month."

I couldn't help it. My jaw dropped. A year? He was dating this lovely person for a year and fucking me just three months ago?

My mind was in a whirl. I felt cheap, I felt used, I felt betrayed. How could he do that? Why did he use me to do that? After what happened with Phoenix, I swore I would never be that person again. And here I was, forced to be that person against my will.

Time seemed to slow down as I tried to process what I should do. Should I out him right then and there? Was that the kind thing to do? There was a slight chance he could have confessed to Ashley and they could have worked it out, but judging by the discomfort clearly written all over his face, that was not the case.

Then Ashley spoke, "If we want to get a beer, one of us should stand in line. I'll go. You talk with Darius and Jess.

I'll be back." Darius went closer to the stage to take pictures of the musician performing.

I waited until I could be sure they were both out of earshot then everything I was feeling poured out of me. "You had a fucking girlfriend?"

"You knew I had a girlfriend when we got together."

"Like hell, I did. How was I supposed to know? You didn't tell me!"

"You didn't ask."

"Uh-uh, no way. You are not putting this on me. If you had told me you had a girlfriend, nothing would have happened, and you know it."

"We were drunk."

"Fuck off, Shawn. Don't put this at my door. You fucked up."

"Are you going to tell her?"

"Oh my god, you're a fucking pussy. No, I'm not going to tell her," I said. "But you have got to own your shit. You have a girlfriend; don't go looking for more women."

I didn't let him answer. I walked away, not caring if Darius was joining me or not.

That interaction put a damper on my day. But somehow, it brought Darius and me closer; we took pictures and even posted to our Instagram feeds, which pre-stories were a big deal. I may have used the tiff as an excuse to drink a few too many nutcrackers that day as well. But overall, Darius helped bring me out of my rut that day.

***

For the next few weeks, I walked around like nothing had happened, like I was in control. I wasn't really. It had really bothered me that Shawn was able to pull the wool over my eyes as much as he did.

"You can't blame yourself," Davey told me. Davey and I met during our first internship at an ad agency. We became close friends after working on a few projects, getting a few happy hours, and so on. I was striking it out on my own and making more than my fair share of mistakes, but at least he was there as some sort of a safety net.

"I mean, I also blame Shawn," I told Davey. "But at the same time, shouldn't I have known?"

"How could you have? Was he shifty at all?"

I tried to recall anything that might have raised a red flag, but I couldn't. Was that because I had red-colored glasses on, or was he truly that deceitful?

"I don't know why you feel you have to put all the blame on your feet."

"I'm not," I said.

"You are," he said firmly. "Would you have slept with him if you knew?"

"No," I knew that much.

"Then why are you beating yourself up?"

I knew why I was beating myself up. Because it was always going to be the girl's fault. That's how it all worked. Everyone always blamed the girl and not the guy. They would have blamed her, thinking she did something wrong to make him stray, and I must have done something nefarious to get him in my grasp. That's how it always was.

"You're not going to be like that, are you, Davey boy?" I leaned into his shoulder. He was safe. He would never do something like that. He smelled amazing.

"Never." He leaned back into me. His cheek was on my head. He was comfortable.

"So what do you want to do?" I finally asked him.

"What do you feel like doing?"

I thought for a moment. He looked at me with his green eyes, cute flushed cheeks, and wide lips. "We could make out."

Shawn's betrayal was forgotten, Davey and I made ourselves comfortable on my couch and had the kind of make out session high school Jess would have told all her friends about.

The beautiful thing was, we were still just friends. Sure, we made out sometimes when there was nothing else to do, and sure, sometimes we had sex, but we were just friends. We didn't have to check in on each other like I would have with a boyfriend. I didn't ask him if he was alright if I went out with the girls, nor did he ask when he went out with the guys.

After supper one night, when we were playing MarioKart, my stomach cramped hard. It was not the right time for my period, and the wave of nausea that rode through me confirmed it was not my period coming early.

My video game character fell off the rainbow road right before I hit the finish line.

"Oh, too bad, so sad, Jess," Davey taunted good-naturedly.

I swatted back at him, willing my stomach to settle down. "Rematch."

Despite my attempts to calm my stomach, nothing seemed to work, and Davey picked up on my discomfort. "Do you want to lie down?"

"Yeah, I think I do."

He wrapped his arms around me, and I lay on my back, taking deep breaths, hoping it would be enough to stop whatever was brewing.

"Do you feel sick?" I asked him. We had both eaten the same fast food.

"I feel fine. Maybe you're pregnant."

"Don't even joke about something like that."

"Just wanted to take your mind off it."

"With my worst nightmare?" I asked.

I continued to breathe deeply and soon fell asleep. Suddenly, I woke up in a panic. The cramps had increased, and I began feeling a build-up of saliva in my mouth. I knew what that meant.

I ran to the bathroom and sat on the toilet, reaching with the speed of the sick for the trash can to vomit in as everything I had ever eaten in my entire life vacated my body as violently as a volcano eruption.

I thanked the universe that Davey's roommate wasn't home but also cursed the universe because I was sweating, puking, and everything else. If I had to be sick like this, why couldn't it have been in the privacy of my own bathroom?

My body was spent, but I didn't trust it, so instead of going back to bed, I lay on the cool tile of the bathroom, feeling relief as it cooled down my body. I begged whatever being was listening for this to be over. If anyone was listening, they didn't give the answer I was hoping for. Curled in the fetal position, I once again began to feel the tell-tale signs of impending vomit. Any strength and accuracy I had was long-gone, and I knew I wouldn't make it to the toilet to vomit in. I heaved myself over the edge of Davey's bathtub, then heaved any remaining contents of my stomach into the white, porcelain tub.

I groaned, my stomach sore and my throat burning, but I couldn't let Davey see me like this. I couldn't let him see his bathroom like this! I turned on the tap and weakly cleaned his tub, making sure all my bilious chunks swirled down the drain. I wasn't surprised my violent vomiting hadn't woken him up; quiet puking had always been a skill of mine. Puke and rally for life.

I spent hours in the bathroom; every time I thought I'd be okay, my body showed me how wrong I was. Finally, after I was certain I had nothing left in me to exit my body, not even tears, I slowly made my way to the bedroom. I stood over Davey and shook his shoulder. "Davey."

His eyes opened immediately. How had he not heard me in the bathroom? "What?"

"I'm really sick. I need to go home right now."

He sat up. "Let's get you a cab, and then I'll get some things for you. Soup, whatever."

I almost melted with how sweet his offer was, but then I remembered the scene in the bathroom. I would rather die than puke or shit in a cab. It's bad enough that I've probably sat on a seat after someone has done that; I don't want to be counted in that number. Plus, there was no way I was going to shit my pants in front of someone I'd slept with. If that happened, I'd have to live in a convent for the rest of my life.

The only option was for him to walk me home. It wasn't a long walk – only 10 or 15 minutes. I could do that.

An hour later, we finally made it into my apartment. It seemed like every five steps or so, I had to stop and puke in the bushes. Or behind a dumpster. Thank God, I only had to puke at this point. Davey made sure I was settled in bed with a bowl within reach. "I'll get you some soup, some soda, Pedialyte, and maybe some crackers. Anything else?"

"A new body," I groaned. "This one's broken."

It was three days before I felt like I wasn't an extra in The Exorcist, and I was ready to face Davey again. "You're fine," he told me when I tried to apologize. "It happens to everyone." "Does it happen to everyone who eats at the chicken spot Jay-z use to work out? Or is this personal?

Sure, being sick happens to everyone, but I don't think everyone has a Davey to help them out. I couldn't remember the last time anyone – much less a guy I wasn't even dating, had treated me so kindly. Davey was someone I'd have to keep around – he was good for the soul.

When Davey's sister came to visit him, I was invited along as he showed her the city. We did typical tourist things, and by the end of the day, all three of us were beat. We decided to stop in at a sushi restaurant that neither Davey nor I had tried yet. We sat beside a window that looked out onto the busy sidewalk, and people watched as we waited for our food.

Davey's sister pointed out a couple who were holding hands and wearing matching sweaters. "Oh, what a cute couple!" she enthused. "I'm going to have to get you two matching shirts."

I froze, a polite smile on my face. Had Davey told his sister we were dating, or had she just assumed we were? I couldn't look at him; I was terrified I'd see something I wasn't ready to see. He was a great guy, but if we dated, then that would be something serious, and I totally wasn't ready for anything serious, even though Davey would be a great guy to be serious with. But I was only 22, definitely not ready for anything remotely serious.

I laughed nervously and pretended to answer a text on my phone. Davey didn't say anything, and neither did his sister. She exclaimed over the food that was brought over two minutes too late to stop her from making that statement in the first place. She didn't even realize the impact her words had made, but I was spooked.

I didn't want him to read too much into things, and I also didn't want to lead him on. Had he caught feelings? Were we too much benefits and not enough friends? Should I talk to him and fully lay out my expectations and his expectations and have a reasonable, grown-up discussion about what was going to happen moving forward? All that sounded like a good thing to do, but I couldn't stop thinking about the what if. What if he wanted a relationship with me? What would I say? Would I say yes because he's Davey and a nice guy, and then I'd be stuck, and then we'd get married, and then I'd have kids, and my life would be over before it really began? Would I say no, and then we wouldn't talk anymore, and one of the best friends I had would be lost to me?

I couldn't take it. My brain was spiraling. I was spiraling. I drew away. We never slept together after his sister visited, and I started finding more and more excuses to avoid seeing him. Soon after I met Mike, and Davey was just a name in my contact list on my phone.

* * *

Mike was eye candy while I dealt with the aftermath of Davey's sister's visit. Going to see bands play that were friends of friends was an easy excuse to avoid Davey. Mike was lean and tall, and I could tell there was an edge to him. He was in a band, after all.

During their breaks between sets, he and his other band members would come sit with their friends. I would make sure the seat closest to me was free, but Mike sat across from me. If I couldn't talk to him, at least I could look at him. He was a little sweaty, which added to his appeal. The tattoos on his knuckles danced in the air while he spoke to his roommate, Robin.

"Oh, yah, Jess does that sort of thing." My ears perked up. Robin was talking about me! I caught his eye and lifted my eyebrow in question. He nodded for me to come over.

"Mike, you know Jess, right? She's come to a couple of your gigs."

"Yah, right. Jess. Good to meet you."

"You guys are pretty great," I said.

"I was just telling Mike that you work in advertising."

"I do," I said.

"Ever do band stuff?" Mike asked.

"Yes, but not since I moved to the city." I didn't want to tell him that the last time I worked on advertising for bands was with my ill-fated high school boyfriend.

Mike just nodded and downed the beer in front of him. I watched his Adam's apple bob as he swallowed. I was entranced. And I had to pee.

"I'll be right back." I gestured to Robin in the area of the bathroom, and he nodded. There was a line to the bathroom, and I debated just holding it so I could get back to Mike, but knew that would be a mistake, so I waited, my impatience growing with each minute.

Finally, I returned to the seat, only to find Mike gone.

"Where's Mike?"

"He's gone."

"But I thought they had another set?"

Robin just shrugged. I sat down beside him. I had missed my chance. I swore I'd never forgive my bladder.

"Hey, cheer up. I'm still here." He wrapped his arm around my shoulder and gave me a light squeeze. Robin was a really nice guy. He wasn't Mike, but Mike was gone. Robin had stayed. Robin always included me in the conversation. Robin was good-looking, though in a different way from Mike. He wasn't as tall as Mike, and he wasn't as lean. His shoulders were broad, and his hands free of tattoos. He had a square jaw, whereas Mike had a narrow jaw. Robin's hair was light brown, whereas Mike's hair was jet-black.

"You want to go back to my place?" I asked him.

He pulled some bills from his pocket and threw them on the table. "Hey, that's for our stuff," he told his friend. "See you later."

He had his arm around my shoulder as we walked home, but as we passed by a Home Depot, Robin stopped. "What's wrong?" I asked.

"Your apartment needs decoration."

"You remember that?" A few weeks ago, I had told him that I had been so busy that my apartment wasn't decorated. I couldn't believe that he remembered something that wasn't even really that important. "What are you going to do?"

In response, he climbed over the fence that was surrounding the Garden Center, shimmying up it like he did it all the time. He moved among the flowers stealthily but with purpose, gathering an array of brightly colored flowers. Then, putting them in his mouth, he climbed back out the way he came.

"No one has stolen flowers for me before," I said after he handed me the flowers and we were on our way.

"Then you're hanging around with the wrong people."

Robin was great in bed, but after, I felt wrong. Not since the time I kissed Phoenix have I felt so badly. Robin was a great guy, but he wasn't the one I wanted to sleep with. Had I slept with him just because he was the first guy I saw after Mike had bailed? Or was it because he had stolen me flowers? And what would happen if Mike found out I slept with his roommate? Would I lose the chance with Mike altogether?

Robin didn't stay the night after we had sex, so I had a lot of time in the dark and the silence to think about what to do. Robin was a great guy, but did I want to do anything else with him? He might not even expect anything. We were both worldly people. We knew what things were and weren't.

I sat up and reached for my phone. Before I lost my nerve or overthought my way out of it, I sent him a text telling him that I had an amazing time, but it wasn't going to go further than that. Then, I sent him another text, asking him if he'd be discreet. I didn't wait for him to respond but turned over my phone so the glowing wouldn't distract me, and I went to sleep, hoping I had done the right thing.

When I woke up the next morning, there was a text on my phone from Robin. He echoed my sentiments and promised he'd be cool about it. The yucky feelings I had felt after he left went away, and I felt lighter. I wanted to promise myself that I wouldn't let myself get into a situation like that, but somehow, deep down, I knew not to make promises I couldn't keep – even to myself.

I saw Robin and Mike several times more as I still attended shows at various bars. Robin was always friendly to me, and I'm sure that to anyone who was observing, all they could see was a friendship, and I was grateful for that. Mike wasn't much of a conversationalist, but he began to notice me more and more. On Friday, I went to the bar, and a girl was there that I didn't recognize. I felt a lump in my throat. I don't know how I knew; I just knew that she was here for Mike. Robin gestured to a seat beside him.

"Who's that?" I asked him.

"Oh, that's Char."

"Char?"

"Mike's girl."

"Oh."

Robin poured me a beer from the pitcher in front of him. "Cheer up! She's not going to be around forever."

How long did Robin know that I had sights on Mike? He must have seen the question on my face because he smiled at me. "All the girls love Mike."

I ignored Mike when he came down after his set. I didn't even notice when Char wrapped her arms around his neck, claiming him as her territory. I didn't see when they made out for almost two minutes at the table. I was calm and suave while I laughed loudly at all the jokes being told – some of them at Mike and Char's expense. I was determined to show Mike that I didn't care, but by the end of the night, I had to admit to myself that Mike didn't care that I didn't care. Why did that make him so much more attractive?

A few months after that night that I first saw Char, I received a text from a number I hadn't saved in my phone. "Hey, it's Mike. Coming to my birthday party?"

Oh my God. Mike texted me. I quickly shot a text to Robin, asking him about Char. Robin responded, texting the news I had been dying for. Char and Mike had broken up. Mike was single. Mike was inviting me to his birthday party. This was my chance!

On the night of Mike's party, I knew I had to play it cool, but not too cool. If I played it too cool, then it would be another couple of months with another Char-like person rubbing herself all over Mike. I wasn't late to the party, but I wasn't on time either. I was wearing my typical outfit: a small, black short sleeve dress and my main accessories – two of my girl friends. I looked good. He looked good. He saw me arrive with a group of friends and ambled over to give me a hug. Oh, God, he gave the best hugs. I wanted to melt into him, but I had to play it cool.

The drinks flowed, the music played, and the dance floor was alive. I had never seen Mike so energized before, but he was talking with everyone, laughing and shouting, moving between people, and making sure to include everyone.

When the last call came, Mike was standing beside me. We talked about getting a cab. "Yes, we should get a cab," He slurred. "You and me, we'll get a cab."

I looked over at my friends, and they gestured for me to go with him.

Drunk Mike was as magnanimous as he was energized. Every time a cab pulled up, he would open the door and encourage someone else from his party to get in. Soon, there weren't many of us left waiting on the street. "Okay, Mike. Let's get this next cab," I said as patiently as I had said it the first time I suggested it.

He nodded his head carefully. I knew the world was spinning for him. He hadn't had to pay for a drink all night, and he had definitely taken advantage of that.

When we sat in the back of the cab, Mike leaned forward as if to give the cabbie his address, but instead, he said, "It's my birthday."

The cabbie was not amused. No doubt he had driven other birthday boys and girls home that night. "What's the address, buddy?"

Mike turned to me. "He's my buddy. You're my buddy."

The cabbie's eyes narrowed. I spoke before he could tell us to get out of the cab. "Bed-Stuy." I gave him my address. Mike crashed into the back of the seat when the cab pulled away from the curb.

"This is why we wear seatbelts," he said. He grabbed my hand, interlaced our fingers, and leaned on my shoulder. This was what I had wanted for so long. Why did he have to be drunk?

I navigated Mike down the hallway to my apartment and then into my bedroom. No matter what I had always wanted, nothing was going to happen between Mike and me that night. I helped him take off his shoes and his leather jacket and made sure there was a glass of water on the bedside table beside him. Then I covered him up and crawled in beside him. Before I fell asleep, he turned over and draped his arm over me, his drunken weight somewhat comforting.

If I had known that I wouldn't see him again after that morning, maybe I would have made more of an effort to talk myself up. I would have flirted more. I would have asked him to hang out in the near future. I would have tried to make concrete plans. But I didn't know I wouldn't see him again, so I just made him coffee. We just talked about surface things. He thanked me for giving him a place to crash, and I told him it was no big deal. Maybe I should have kissed him, or at least given him strong signals that I wanted him to kiss me. When he stood at the door and gave me a hug more chaste than two junior high students, I thought I'd have more opportunities to shoot my shot. I was wrong, and the image of him walking down the hallway trying to find the elevator is the last memory I have of him.

——-

I can't end this early chapter of my life without one of the most valuable lessons I have learned. If you are hungover, and I mean the real kind IYKYK, don't wear a dress. And certainly do not wear a white dress. You may find yourself with a dead phone, no way to call a car after an errand, and what's now a full stomach of sewage.

You may then find yourself walking as fast as you can without separating your legs in a white dress on a Sunday morning, sweating out the pain of the situation of holding your shit in for dear life. You'll get closer and closer to your home and sweat more and more. Don't do this to yourself. Learn from others' mistakes.

# And I'm Only 23

Every year on my birthday, I reflect on the year just ending and look forward to what my life will look like. Here I was in New York City, living my dream. Sure, I wasn't having the best of luck with men, but it wasn't as if I was having terrible luck either. I had some great times with some great guys. I wasn't looking to settle down, not at 23. I wanted to have fun.

The morning after my birthday, I woke up hungover. I splashed water on my face and watched the water drip down into the sink. I was having fun. I was having the same kind of fun men had been having for years. I thought about Lisa, who had been far more conservative than the rest of my friends. She and I lost touch a couple of years after high school. I wondered what she would think, then I shook that thought off. Who cared what she thought? There were two options. Either she would look down on me and my "lifestyle," or she had done what a lot of uptight girls did and gone completely off the deep end. It didn't matter. It didn't matter what anyone thought. I was living the life I wanted to live. I was fine with everything. Well, most things. I could go without the cheating men, the abusive men, and the creepy men.

23 was going to be my year. Maybe I would move to Portland – I had seen a job posting. Portland could be nice. I decided then and there that I would apply for that job. What's the worst thing that could happen? If they turned me down, I'd still be living in New York, and I loved New York.

# 23: The Year of Jess!

***

I loved frequenting the Cobra Club. The Cobra Club is a unique hybrid venue that's a coffee shop, bar, performance space, and yoga studio. The crowd had a similar vibe to me and my friends; it was sort of punk rock metal, and the bridge/tunnel/Manhattan crowd rarely bothered to venture into this dive bar. One night, while sitting at the bar enjoying a few glasses of vodka soda, I saw an attractive man a few seats down. He was drumming his fingers on the bar in tune with the music and casually looking at his phone. He had dark blond hair, almost brown, and wore black jeans and a black t-shirt advertising for a rock band I'd never heard of. He was nice to look at, and he seemed to be so involved with his phone, I wasn't worried about him catching me every time I felt like looking at him again. It wasn't just that he was good-looking; there was something else about him, some other attractive quality that I just couldn't put my finger on. It could have been the way he wore his hair, it could have been his tattoos and where he chose to put them. It could have been a combination of things; did it matter?

I was too nervous to approach him despite it being the Year of Jess, but every time I went to the Cobra Club, I would check the room to see if he was there. He seemed to always sit in the same spot, drinking the same drink and looked at his phone. He was a bit of a mystery, and that added to his charm.

It was weeks after I first saw him when I finally built up the courage to speak to him. I finished my drink and placed it on the high-top table where a group of us was gathered around. "I'm going for a smoke," I told the person beside me. They nodded, and I stepped around the groups of people that had gathered. It was later in the evening, and the bar was getting crowded as the band playing that night was setting up.

I walked past a short line of smokers while grabbing a cigarette out of its pack. When I lit it and took that first inhale, I saw that my mystery man was beside me. Had he always been there, or was this part of his mystery? I decided the universe was telling me now was my time, and I was determined to do what the universe said.

"Hey," I said in what I hope was a chill, not-at-all thirsty-tone.

He looked at me, then looked up and down at me while he exhaled. Oh my God, how was that so hot? "How's it going?"

"I'm pretty good. Looking forward to the band. I heard them play a few months ago."

"Yeah, they're good." He nodded and took another drag.

"I'm Jess," I said.

"Chad." The blare of a car horn smothered what he said after his name.

"What?" I said.

"You came here by yourself?"

"No. I'm with some friends. You?" I asked.

"I come here by myself all the time." Like I didn't know that. "How else can I get pretty girls to talk to me?"

Oh, I see how it is, Mr. Chad. Let's do this. "It's a solid plan," I said laughing. "How's it working out for you?"

"So far so good, Jess." Was it just me, or did he put an emphasis on my name? He pointed to my cigarette butt; my cigarette long gone. "You need to go back inside?"

I took another cigarette out of the pack. "I still need to finish my cigarette.

"Uh-huh," he said, taking another long drag, his eyes not leaving mine.

I tried to will my cigarette to burn slowly, but it seemed like it was the fastest burning cigarette in the world. I didn't want to light another one – I wasn't a chain smoker. "I should get back to my friends. Talk to you later, though, yeah?"

Chad stood still. "Talk to you later."

By the time I made it back to the table, the band had started to play and the lights had dimmed. "Where were you?" my friends asked.

I leaned in and told them about Chad. They had all known about the mystery man, and every single one of them was excited for me that I had finally gotten his name. I told them about how he looked at me, and they all exchanged glances. "Girl, you're going home with him," Lucy told me.

"I am not!" I protested. "I literally just found out his name." None of them spoke; their disbelief clearly registered on their faces. "Fine! He's coming home with me."

Lucy led the group in a cheer, followed by laughter. I looked over my shoulder to what I had begun to think of as Chad's spot, and there he was. "Go, Jess; you know you want to."

I listened to the band for a few moments, knowing my friends were dying to just push me away from the table but wanting them to suffer a little bit. When the band finished the song, I grabbed my phone and my purse. "Alright, see you later."

I knew the universe was definitely looking out for me when the chair beside Chad's spot was empty. Not wanting to tempt fate, I quickly sat down. "Hey Chad."

Chad smiled at me, and I knew I wasn't just blowing smoke. He had gorgeous laugh lines around his eyes. "Hi Jess." He didn't say another word but waved to the bartender and asked for his tab. Once he paid, he said, "Do you want to get out of here?"

"Let's go."

My apartment wasn't far from the Cobra Club, and I knew it would be empty tonight. We walked with intention, our pace fast but not too fast. I still couldn't put my finger on what made him so attractive, but I had fun uncovering every bit of him trying to figure out what it was.

He ran his hands all over my body, much like his eyes had run over them when we stood outside smoking. My skin prickled at his touch, and I was eager for him to get inside me.

The next morning, we both were feeling the effects of the loud bar, and neither of us was feeling too eager to get out of bed. He was lying on his stomach, his head resting on his arms. I saw that a tattoo covered his entire back – a dragon with a devilish face, and I ran my fingers along it, tracing out the shape. His skin rose under my touch, and he shivered. "Oh, are you ticklish?" I teased, not letting up.

In a flash, he rolled over and caught my wrists in his hands. "Let's see how ticklish you are," he said, tormenting me more than I had done him.

"What are you doing today?" I asked, out of breath from laughing.

"No plans," he said, sliding out of bed and pulling up his pants. I pulled on a nearby t-shirt as he buttoned his own. "Well, actually, yeah, there is something, but you know."

I didn't know, but I didn't push him, even though I really did want to know. He kissed me, gently grabbing a handful of my hair, and then left. We hadn't made plans, and I didn't know if I would see him again. Whatever, it was fine. Completely and totally fine.

It was totally and completely fine, I told myself every time I got a text notification, and it wasn't him. It was what it was. There are other guys, and it's totally okay if we had a one-night stand. I had fun, I know he had fun. It was fine.

After two weeks of being totally and completely fine, I got a text message from him inviting me to his art show. His art show? I didn't remember him saying he was an artist. Maybe that was part of the appeal – I've always been drawn to creatives. But he was inviting me. That was a good sign. It didn't matter that there had been two weeks of silence beforehand. Creatives are flaky; I knew that. I was creative.

I was too proud to tell anyone how excited I was to go to the art show and see Chad. I had worked hard to portray this cool girl who didn't cling and was totally fine with letting things go the way they went. I just couldn't help myself with Chad. I walked into the bar/studio, where his show was full of butterflies. My face felt hot, and I prayed that it wasn't as red as it felt. It didn't take me long to find him in the crowd, but he wasn't alone. Beside him was a beautiful, no, a gorgeous woman. She was taller than me and skinnier than me. Her skin was immaculate, and she was wearing an amazing dress. I thought about turning around and going home, but he had invited me. That had to mean something, right?

"Hey," I said brightly, maybe too brightly. Dial it back, Jess.

"Jess, hi!" he said, giving me a chaste hug. That wasn't a good sign. "This is Amanda. She's my best friend." I was holding my breath, and now I had to let it go without anyone knowing I had been holding my breath.

Amanda smiled at me and shook my hand. "Nice to meet you." I knew that Chad had introduced Amanda as his friend, and there's no way she would be okay with him saying that if they were more than friends. I would not be okay with being introduced as friends if we were more than that. All the same, I was jealous. I couldn't help it.

Chad excused himself, saying there was someone else he wanted to say hi to. Amanda and I laughed awkwardly, then she floated away to another group, seamlessly joining their conversation. I stood there like a fish out of water, feeling like a complete idiot.

Chad hadn't wanted me there because we had mind-blowing sex and he wanted to develop something more. He wanted me there because he wanted more people at his art show. He probably texted everyone in his contact list.

I eyed the exit with longing, wondering if I had to stay for any speech or anything. Deciding I didn't care if I did miss a speech, I made a move for the door but was intercepted by Chad.

"You're leaving?"

"Yup," I said.

"Are you upset?" His brow furrowed, and his eyes darkened. Could he really be that stupid?

"Yes. I am," I told him, then left without giving him a chance to reply. I was afraid if I did give him a chance then he would be able to charm me into staying. I didn't want to be that girl. I wasn't desperate. I didn't need him. There were plenty of other guys out there.

I walked home faster than usual, my anger giving me speed. I hadn't planned on coming home this early or this solo. I had fully expected Chad to see me, realize he had missed me, and I'd take him home again. Or maybe he'd take me home.

Instead, I was sitting at home in an outfit that was far frumpier than the dress Amanda had worn, swiping through my dating app. For every right swipe, there were probably 10 or more left swipes, but there was nothing else to do, thanks to Chad and his idiocy.

I matched with Paul, and we immediately started texting. He wasn't doing anything tonight either, and since I was already dressed up, we made plans to meet.

We met at a classic bar. It's gone now, but the Wreck Room was dirtier than any bar I had ever been to. Bathrooms didn't have gender markers (which didn't bother me), the stalls didn't have doors, and if the bathroom sinks didn't overflow, then the toilets did. The bar area upstairs consisted of bar stools, a broken table and booth, and car seats that had been ripped out of a car. I felt more relaxed there then I had at that stuffy art studio. Stupid Chad.

Not too long after, just a few days, my upstairs neighbor rang the doorbell looking for my roommate, who wasn't home. So Greg offered to share the bottle of wine in his hand with me. I couldn't let him drink alone; that'd just be rude. So we drank together.

We hooked up and continued to do so for the next few weeks. He was beginning to want something more serious, while I, on the other hand, did not want that at all. So, we decided to break off anything before it became serious, and I had fallen into a pattern of dating another man…named Greg during this time. We'll call him Greg 2. We had several successful dates until he joined the typical male dating trend of 'ghosting.' I decided it was time to get over him and under someone else.

Paul was in a band. He played guitar, but unlike Adam, Paul seemed far more accomplished, or at least that's what he had said.

"We've been playing for several years. Of course, when we started, it was mostly our friends and family coming to our gigs, but now we have a pretty decent fan base."

I liked Paul, and not just because he wasn't Chad. That first date went so well we immediately planned for a second one, and then after that, a third one, after which we had sex.

The honeymoon period didn't last long, however. It was dawning on me that Paul had more optimism than realism. When he told me his band played a lot, he should have said they played in rehearsal. I wanted to ask him why they spent more time rehearsing than they did trying to get bookings, but I didn't want to find myself in another Happy Aliens! situation where I was doing all these things for the band just because I was sleeping with the guitar player.

I was busy at work, and it seemed we could go weeks without seeing one another. He wasn't the worst at texting, but I wanted a boyfriend, not a pen pal.

One night, while Paul was in rehearsal and I was walking Buttercup, the phone rang. It was Leif, a guy I ran into at a pub who looked like he had jumped out of an anime program. On the night we went out, he got me drunk, reneged on his promise to take me to dinner, and took advantage of me. I left his place and got on the train, but was so sick, I threw up between train cars at the first stop. I never wanted to see Leif again, and it wasn't as if he was pursuing me after he got what he wanted.

"Hello?"

"Hey, it's Leif."

"What do you want?"

"Uh, look. This isn't easy to say."

"What, that you were an asshole? Seems pretty easy for me to say."

"I have chlamydia. And… I probably gave it to you, so you should get tested." At this point, it felt like there was a hive of bees in my head, my ears were buzzing so loud. Of all the things I thought he could have said, I never would have expected that.

"Fuck me!" I shrieked just before I ended the phone call. Buttercup barked in response, and several people turned to stare at me. Tourists.

I had never had an STI scare before. Buttercup, and I turned around and I hurried back home. I needed to make an appointment with a clinic. I needed to sit down. I needed to breathe.

I was lucky and managed to get an appointment for the middle of the week – that was only three days away. I could wait three days. Three days were nothing.

After waiting one day, I went to Dr. Google and WebMD. I learned I was going to die. Not from chlamydia; that was totally curable. No, I was going to die because I had to tell Paul if I had it.

I paced around my apartment for the next two days. I could barely concentrate on work. I couldn't tell Paul. How was I supposed to tell Paul? Paul and I got along really well; he was a very chill person. Maybe he wouldn't be that upset. Maybe I didn't even have chlamydia. Maybe I was worrying over nothing.

Two days later, I had reason to worry. I did have chlamydia, and the horse-sized pills I was given to get rid of it were not the hardest pill to swallow. Now, I had to tell Paul.

I sent him a text. Hey, want to hang out and talk? It probably would have been easier for me to tell him over text, but I couldn't do that. Telling someone they might have chlamydia deserved an in-person conversation, not a text and not being ambushed with a phone call.

Paul and I made plans to go for supper that night. I dressed up in an outfit I knew he would like and waited for him to text me that he was at my apartment.

Every time my phone dinged with a notification, my heart jumped, but it was never Paul. 20 minutes after we had agreed to meet, I texted him, but there was no response. Two hours after we had agreed to meet, I called him, but there was no response. I still sat and paced and sat again, my nerves wreaking havoc on my body.

I couldn't stand it any longer, and I couldn't wait up. It was late, and I needed to work in the morning. As much as I wanted to rip this bandage off, I had to go to bed. I was in the middle of brushing my teeth when my phone pinged with a text notification from Paul.

"Sorry, last-minute band practice and it went late."

"Last-minute band practice? Who are they practicing for? The crowd of no one who has heard of him?"

I responded, "Alright, well we had plans and that was really shitty but whatever. I just wanted to meet up to let you know something."

I didn't want to tell him over text, but I knew I couldn't sleep without telling him. It wasn't my fault; this was how he was going to find out. He was the one who decided to bail on me.

I have chlamydia, and you need to get tested. I turned my phone over after I sent that text. My heart pounded. I turned the phone back over and looked at the message screen. He had read the message. There were three dots, so I knew he was writing something. Or maybe he was leaving me on read. I would be okay if he left me on read. I would be okay if I never talked to him again. That would probably be easier for both of us.

Then my phone buzzed again. He hadn't left me on read. He had left me a novel.

You goddamn whore, who were you sleeping with that gave you that? I know I didn't. What the fuck, Jess, are you so desperate for love that you'll spread your legs for any janky guy that looks at you? I can't believe I ever thought you were cool; you're just like all the other girls who have sex with anyone. And way to go, by the way, for making me have sex with you. Wait a second, Paul, what? He was the one who suggested we have sex on our third date. I wasn't falling over him with my breasts hanging out. The text went on. And what if it's more than chlamydia. What if you fucking gave me AIDS, you dirty bitch. You like that? You like that I could be dying now because of you and because you can't keep people out of your pants? You are a horrible person, and it's your fault I didn't wear a condom. You whore. You fucking dirty cheating whore.

I wanted to laugh off his words, but they came out in a sob. The torrent of viciousness was too much for me. How could anyone be so awful? We had both made mistakes. We should have worn a condom but I didn't force him, and he didn't force me. We were mutually stupid. I tried to stop the tears from coming. I didn't want his words to affect me so much. If that's the type of man he was, then I didn't want to cry over him. He didn't deserve the effort.

Buttercup curled in a ball into my lap as I cried. I couldn't stop, so I decided to just let them come. I cried because of Paul's awful words; I cried because I had chlamydia; and I cried because I needed to cry.

When I finished crying, I picked up my phone again. Paul was not going to have the last word. Not with those words.

Calm the fuck down. You're not dying; just go to the doctor. After I pressed send, I blocked his number and removed him from my contact list. I vowed to never let anyone else speak to me like that.

After my course of azithromycin was complete, I was hesitant to get back into the dating world. I wouldn't have admitted it out loud, but Paul's words shook me up more than I would have liked. It was frightening how quickly he turned on me. What would have happened if I had told him in person? Would he have become violent? When I thought about it, I felt sick. So far, the Year of Jess was not going as well as I had hoped.

Then I received an email about the job I had applied for in Portland. They wanted to interview me! I had almost forgotten I had applied, and if I hadn't gotten chlamydia, I probably wouldn't have gone through with the interview, but I needed a change. Layla was interviewing me. She was from London, England, and had made the leap to Portland. She and I got along swimmingly in my interview, and I knew we would get along well. I began thinking that this contract would be a great idea and a great move for my career and for my personal life. I knew I could learn a lot from Layla. My interview went well, and they offered me the job. I was moving from New York to Portland!

I hated Portland. The first two weeks I was there, I only saw six people of color, and four of them were in the same family. I missed the diversity of New York. I missed the clubs of New York. The food in Portland was okay, but was it enough to get me to stay?

I stayed in a hotel for the first week in Portland, despite my contract stating the job would arrange for an apartment for me to stay at. I didn't want to wait for the company and moved into an Airbnb rental. It was a small row of houses, all Airbnb's by the same middle-aged couple. They seemed very hippish and spent most of their time watering the gardens or sitting in them. The other guests in the units near me were nice and always said hi as Buttercup and I passed but none of them interested me enough to bother to start a conversation. Some of them also had dogs and some did not.

Lonely and missing the lights and noise of New York, I explored some of the pubs and bars near my place. I had always been extroverted in New York, but it was harder for me to start conversations with strangers. I sometimes felt like I was in a completely different country that had different customs. If it weren't for Layla, I'm sure I'd have no girlfriends at all there.

One night, while sitting at a bar and wishing someone would come talk to me, someone did.

"You new here?" a man asked. He was around my age and only an inch or so taller than me. He looked like a typical Portland man. He had a stubbly beard with plastic-framed glasses and wore dark khaki pants and a knit sweater.

"Is it that obvious?" I asked.

"Only to people with eyes," he was teasing. I liked when guys teased me.

"I'm Jess," I said and shook his hand. He had a warm, firm grip. I liked when guys had a warm, firm grip.

"Trevor."

"What do you do?"

"I'm a pilot."

"I think that's the first time I've met a pilot," I told him. He took the chair next to me and asked if he could buy me a drink.

Trevor was sweet and earnest. I liked spending time with him; it made the other dramas that surrounded my life a bit more bearable.

My parents flew out to visit me. Neither of them had been to Portland before, and I was more than a little happy to see some familiar faces.

I mentioned my parents' visit in passing to Stella, the landlady of the Airbnb. She had always seemed quirky, but was always nice to Buttercup and me.

"It's nice your parents are coming out to visit you. Where are they staying?"

"Oh, they're staying here."

Stella's demeanor shifted. "They can't."

I thought she was joking and laughed awkwardly. "What?"

"No visitors allowed."

"That wasn't in the contract."

Stella's entire body stiffened, and she took a deep breath. I winced, afraid of what was going to come out of her mouth. "No visitors allowed; I make the rules; that's the rule. If I find out you have visitors…"

I cut her off. "Look, I don't know what you're talking about, but I've never not been allowed to have visitors. I'm going to take a look at my contract and call Airbnb to help me sort this out."

I quickly typed an email to Airbnb customer support and looked out the window. Stella hadn't moved. She was staring up at the window with her hands on her hips. I've never seen that level of crazy outside the city. She could give some people I'd encountered in New York a run for their money. She reached into her pocket and took out her phone. I hoped that was Airbnb telling her she was out of line.

I got out my computer and resumed work on the project I had been contracted for that brought me to Portland in the first place – it was a three-month contract working on a large client as well as filling in on a few other projects. It was meant to be temporary to permanent, but I was not looking at it as a permanent option.

When I work, I get into a groove, and I am always surprised at how much time has passed. When my phone rang, I had been at it for almost an hour.

An Airbnb representative was on the other end of the call, with concern in their voice. "You have to move right now."

"What? This is ridiculous. I should be allowed to have people over." I was ready to die on this hill.

"I'm telling you this is a matter of safety. This woman is threatening to kill your dog. Get away from there as soon as you can, and we will do what we can to resolve your account on your end."

What the hell was this place? Work forgotten, I frantically looked online for any available hotel rooms. Just my luck, there was a conference in town, and the only rooms available were in a Motel 6. Normally, I'd avoid places like that, but Buttercup's life was at stake, and I'd do anything for her, even stay at a Motel 6.

I didn't know how long I could handle living here. The work I was doing wasn't even enjoyable. Even working with Layla wasn't enough to keep me going.

Layla's partner at the agency was a man named Phil. He walked around like he was a prince of Portland and had disgusting business practices. The project I had been contracted for had been full of stress since the beginning. As my contract was winding down and deadlines were approaching, Phil became more and more unbearable. He would berate me in front of my team, as well as other members of my team. He insisted we weren't working hard enough, then walked out of the office promptly at 3 p.m. each day.

We had a computer crash when the deadline was down to the wire, and my entire team stayed awake for 40 hours in an attempt to finish the project and fix the crash. We were able to finish in time for Phil to fly to LA with the deliverables in hand. Despite my exhaustion, despite living in a Motel 6, I was elated. There's always a sense of pride I got when I finished a project, especially one as stressful as this one. I felt powerful. It was a huge step in my career pulling off such a feat.

When Phil returned, he called me into his office. Layla wasn't there.

"Jess, I have to say, I'm disappointed with how all this turned out."

I nodded, thinking he was going to apologize for the stress he had caused. "Agreed."

"What happened with the computer was completely unacceptable."

Wait. Was he blaming me? It sounded like he was ramping up to blame me.

"Your team should not have been working the hours they did. It seems to me you weren't able to properly manage them."

"We had an unforeseen glitch, and we worked to ensure it would not negatively impact the client."

Phil waved his hands like he was pushing away my logic. "I think you'll understand that it's best we don't renew your contract here." Stunned, I left his office. Was the man who probably weighed over 300 pounds and took me to a strip club my first dinner in Portland really blaming me?? I had never been so undervalued in a contract. This job wasn't my dream job, and Portland was not the place I wanted to end my life, but there was no way I was to blame for anything that went wrong on that project.

I vented to Trevor on the phone that night. If there was any bright spot in the dark void that was Portland, it was Trevor. He understood my insane hours, and he was always willing to listen to me. When things got too stressful, he would take me out to the movies or to a bar.

"Jess, that sucks so much. You've worked so hard for that company. It's not right that they treat you like that."

"So, now I get to figure out what I'm going to do."

"I'll tell you what you can do tomorrow."

"What's that?"

"Come to my place. I'm having a small get-together. I'll have some vegetarian food just for you."

When I got to his place the next day, Trevor was already tipsy. He threw his arms around me and gleefully introduced me as his girlfriend to everyone who was there. Girlfriend? I wasn't even sure I was going to stay much longer. I didn't want to have to deal with relationship drama on top of everything.

While making the necessary rounds as Trevor introduced me to everyone, I noticed a large sheet cake.

When I got close enough, I could see the word. "Congratulations!" was written on it with blue lettering and the image of an airplane in icing.

"What is this?" I asked Trevor.

"I graduated!" he exclaimed. He pulled me close for a hug and spun me around. "Can you believe it! I finally have my pilot's license. Everything is perfect. I have the perfect job, the perfect girlfriend, whom I love. I cannot wait to get married and have kids."

I pulled away from him. Love? Marriage? Kids? I hadn't even known him for three months. I had to get out of there. I was afraid he was going to spring a proposal on me.

The next morning, I called Trevor and called it off. The following week, I turned 24, and I didn't have a job, didn't have an apartment, and didn't have enough friends to celebrate.

I found a donut shop, bought six donuts, and ran myself a bath. I couldn't even have a bubble bath. I had a normal bath in the off-white bathtub of a Motel 6, where I ate all six donuts, dyed my hair red/black and watched the Jinx with Buttercup.

23 wasn't the Year of Jess despite all my hopes and plans. It was a disaster, but I knew one thing. I was going home to New York.

# And I'm Only 24

Back in New York, I breathed in the air that I had missed when I was in Portland. How could I ever think there was any other place for me than here?

I didn't have any plans for my belated 24th birthday; I didn't really have a lot to celebrate. I had such a bad time in Portland, it was hard to just bounce back. It was still my birthday, however, so I went out with a few friends, just to mark the occasion. By the end of the night, it was only my cousin celebrating with me.

"Oh my God, Jess!"

"What?" we had to yell to hear each other over the music.

"I know what I'm going to get you for your birthday!"

I was intrigued. "What?"

"I'm going to get you laid!" She dissolved into laughter and swigged back the rest of her drink.

"Let's do it!" I said. I would love to have birthday sex.

After a cursory look around at the men at the club we were at, she decided there was no one there good enough for her to present to me.

"Not here!" she said. "Let's go somewhere else."

After settling our tab at the bar, I led her to a local dive bar. My cousin was a woman on a mission and practically held interviews for the role of a birthday lay. Finally, she had found some contenders. They weren't amazing, but at some point, my cousin had to concede she wasn't going to find the perfect birthday lay. She picked out a guy for me and a guy for her, and as we were walking home, we learned they were from Staten Island. My cousin and I exchanged a look. This wasn't ideal, but we could close our eyes and imagine they were someone better.

When we got to my apartment, my cousin and I went to our separate rooms, and I prepared for birthday sex with this guy, whom I began to realize was now almost too drunk to stand. I could barely stand to kiss him; his lips were sloppy against mine, and the fumes from all the beers he had consumed that night were enough to intoxicate a giant.

Still, it was my birthday, and I wanted birthday sex. Our clothes came off, and foreplay was on. Then suddenly, he stopped moving. "What's wrong?" I asked him.

He held up his hand, then it flew to his mouth as his cheeks bulged. He practically pushed me off the bed as he ran to the bathroom, where I heard the most disgusting vomiting sounds I've ever heard. I almost vomited when I heard him. I peeked around the corner to see the worst mess anyone could make. He hadn't been able to make it to the toilet, but he was able to make it to the wall, floor, sink, and pretty much every part of the bathroom that wasn't the toilet.

"Get out!" I screamed.

"What?" he moaned.

"Get the fuck out!"

He slowly put on his clothes as if he was expecting me to change my mind. I stood, arms crossed across my naked chest, as he finally got everything of his and left the apartment. I stood in the doorway of the bathroom, surveying the mess. "Happy birthday, Jess." I wanted this to be better than the last few months had been. I wanted it to be a kind of restitution for what I had to put up with in Portland. Instead, I let my cousin – as well-meaning as she had meant to be – convince me to sleep with a guy who I didn't find particularly attractive, from Staten Island, and who made the worst mess I had ever seen in my life! Was this indicative of what my whole year would be like?

I cleaned the bathroom with the help of my cousin, who had heard a bit of the commotion and kicked the other Staten Islander out. My year had to be better. It just had to be!

***

I was lucky enough to find myself with another job, not a contract, but a full-time job! I was being brought into an experiential team, which was brilliant because events had always been a huge interest and goal of mine to conquer. I was originally brought on to help with digital activations within the event, but the team was far too understaffed for the projects coming in, so I wore multiple hats. I'd been working on a project for an outdoor clothing company for about a month, planning, presenting, and putting into action the events needed to make the activation happen. But one morning I was lying on my couch, playing with Buttercup, when my phone rang. It was my mom. Phone calls with my mother were always filled with the mundane before she got to the reason for her call.

"How has your day been? Did you know that Hannah joined a horseshoe league and she's winning? We'll be planning to go to the cabins sometime after my birthday. I'm going to make ribs and mashed potatoes for dinner. Also, I heard Grandma died."

How did she know before I did? Gran and I lived in the same city – shouldn't I have known first? I gathered Buttercup in my arms, breathed in her comforting scent, and cried for the woman who gave me a place to stay when I first moved here. She was a force, and I was proud to be her great granddaughter.

My parents even flew in for the funeral. A true Catholic funeral lasts for days, and boy did this one. Nearly the whole small town of Oyster Bay and surrounding towns came, especially if they'd ever attended the church that she had cooked at for nearly 40 years. There was a reason she lived on church property so long, even after retiring. Nearly the whole family showed up, outside of my own grandfather, who had cut me out of his life many years prior, though I was a kid who had no say in family matters. But, honestly, that was a relief. We didn't need any drama at this wonderful, caring, big-hearted woman's funeral.

I felt my phone buzz in my purse, but I ignored it, focusing on the picture of my gran surrounded by flowers.

On the final day of the wake, the smaller group, mostly family and very close friends, watched Grandma be buried in the cemetery nearby. We were going to go to a small family dinner at the nearby restaurant she loved, which we were only allowed to take her to on her birthday. She very much still acted like the Great Depression was upon us when it came to money and spending it out on food when we could get a home-cooked meal from her. So in her honor, we went there. My dad and I left early to get a break from family but also to let Buttercup out. When we got home, there was blood all over the floor.

We rushed her to the hospital, now nearing 11 p.m. at night. I was uncontrollably crying at the thought of another death I just couldn't handle. After what seemed like hours, we were seen. My poor Buttercup had a UTI, and it was a bad one; she must have felt our stress, so she didn't make a fuss about it. Luckily, we were able to get her help.

My parents left the next morning early, and we all went about our days. It took months for me to not think at times of boredom to call Grandma and just hear her voice and ask how she's doing, then I'd remember she wouldn't answer.

On that first day alone, thinking about calling her out of habit – I remembered that my phone had been buzzing earlier and took it from my purse after I snubbed out my cigarette. It was the office. Sal, a young kid fresh out of college, was frantically messaging me, saying something was going on with the project. I'd been gone just under a week from work, and apparently things had really hit the fan, and we were a week out from activation. No one had ever called in event insurance. I was in trouble, the company was in trouble, the project was at risk, and the client couldn't find out.

My grandmother had just died; I couldn't deal with what Sal was saying. Wasn't there anyone else who could step in and take action?

When I came back to work the next day, my boss called me into her office. She detailed everything that had gone wrong, like I hadn't already heard about it from Sal and every other member of the team. "This is absolutely unacceptable. You needed to be on top of things."

"I'm sorry this happened, Cheryl," I said. "As you know, I was out of the office at a funeral. There wasn't anything I could have done."

"Nevertheless," she said. "I will have to make note of this in your file."

I left her office fuming. This was being put on my file, but none of my achievements would ever be noted. Additionally, the project had been left in her hands with a detailed handoff of the status of everything. I was new; I'd never even spoken to her insurance agent, and she gave me no introduction – surprisingly, to this day, I still can't read people's minds. I rejoined my team, and together, we fixed what wasn't working and strengthened what was. I was proud of our final result. Despite all the stress, it was these achievements that made me love what I did and look forward to getting the project back on track. We did, and we had a great two weeks of activation. We made great content in post-production, and I got to see a lot of America (New York to Utah, to be exact). We got back, and I reconciled the job. On budget and on time. I felt good.

Before I could start another project the next week, that Friday, Cheryl called me into her office again. "This obviously isn't a fit for us, Jessica." I wanted to slam my hand on her desk. My name wasn't Jessica!

"I don't understand," I said instead.

"We can't have you leaving the office at a time when a project needs you."

"I'm sorry, were you talking about when I was at my grandmother's funeral?"

"I'm sure there were other times as well." She waved her hand imperiously.

There weren't any other times. "I have worked late several nights a week working on this project," I reminded her.

"Jessica…"

"It's Jess," I interrupted.

She looked down her nose at me. "If you're not able to adapt to the time commitments this job demands, then maybe this isn't the career for you."

"I just want to be clear," I said, but she wouldn't let me finish.

"Yes, let's make this clear. Please hand over your access card and give Sal access to your files. We're letting you go."

There was no point in arguing. Her mind was made up. I dropped my access card on her desk, and it bounced once before settling down. Instead of sending Sal any files, I threw my work computer across the room, grabbed my things, and ran out the door before my tears began to stream down my face.

I made my way to the nearest park, sat on the first empty bench I could find, curled into a ball, and cried. In between bursts of emotion, I texted my roommate to tell her what had happened and cried until she found where I was and took me on the L train home, still sobbing, as a true New Yorker would. Because who fucking cares what anyone thinks.

The next day, I woke up, brushed myself off, and looked for the next opportunity. I was resilient. I had to be; there was no other option. I convinced Leah to go out with me. You know at this age when a friend is upset, in the dumps, and ready to drink/party, they're taking you down with them. And I did just that; we met up with some of her promoter friends, danced, drank, sniffed, and repeated. By the end of the night, I was swaying drunkenly on a mutual friend, Nick, of Leah's and the lead promoters. Who happened to be recently engaged. Leah decided it was time to go.

However, Nick and I had each other's numbers from a previous night, and throughout the cab ride, I was able to somehow type her address and sneak out to "smoke." It didn't take Leah long to figure out what was happening; she came downstairs from her apartment to find me making out with Nick. I had not only brought her to my drunk level, I had brought him down to my level of bullshit and risked his happy future life. I wasn't planning on changing, but I was planning on not allowing that specific make-out session to happen again.

It was nearing the holidays, and I was upset to be unemployed in a tough world, so I bought a one-way ticket to Europe to visit my dearest friend Annie. One day her (then) husband asked what I'd do during the day while they were at work. I had no idea; I'd been to Glasgow a few times and seen the majority of the museums and other touristy things to see, so I just sort of shrugged. He suggested I take a train and the boat to the Isle of Arran. A beautiful island with a castle and lots of hiking. So, without hesitation and a pair of sneakers, I did just that. While I was hiking the flatlands but gorgeous area of the Isle, I saw a man in a kilt painting with his dog. I asked if I could eat my sad lunch near them and to watch him paint. He agreed, we began talking, and he asked, "So, are you going to climb the mountain?"

"Mountain, what mountain?"

He gestured up and over, and there it was, a snow-covered mini-mountain. He went on to tell me it's one of the easiest in the world to climb, and I'd be able to do it and be back in town in time for dinner and the boat, easily. So I parted with the man and his dog and began my journey up a hill…up a mountain, I suppose.

I was tired; my legs hurt, but I was tired of crying over a short-term job and stupid boys, so I hiked forward. Mind you, I had indeed gone to the gym a ton in my 20s, but I had never planned or trained to climb a mountain. Once I hit the snow, I ran into two hikers who had backpacks filled with food and water, real winter jackets, and even snow shoes. I was clearly doing this wrong.

They told me I was super close to the top and to keep going; I could follow their snowshoes down on my way back down. I got to what felt like it had to be the top; I was in the clouds after all. I took a picture of gray and sat for a moment to catch my breath.

I realized when I went to get up that my legs DID NOT WORK. I mean it, I'd never used my legs this way, and they just didn't move forward; I actually climbed a majority of the way down with my arms. I had tried to dial the emergency services, but I had no service on the top of a mountain. The snowshoe prints were gone thanks to the wind and snow. But I somehow made it down and began the path toward the castle – which was in the direction of the boat.

All of a sudden I was in a forest, I couldn't see the castle, it was getting dark, and I was completely lost. By some weird act of the goddesses, I heard humans, and they too sounded lost.

I found them after a short bend in the road; it was a mother, father, and two small children. I spoke to them in English; only the father could speak English, they were from Poland. I found out they too had gotten lost and that we were nearing the time of the last boat. We decided to head in the direction where he and I felt might be the right direction. We finally made it out of the woods to find ourselves in a sea of cow fields. We had no time to think; he jumped one fence, and I handed him over one kid at a time, then his wife. We did this through several fields until we finally made it to the main road. Catching the last bus which took us to the last boat of the day. We made it to the dock, thanked each other, and said our goodbyes.

I got on the boat and realized I had climbed a fucking mountain. I knew I could go home to New York City knowing and carrying that with me for the rest of my life. I wasn't quite ready to go home yet and still hadn't bought my ticket back. Annie and I had found last-minute day of tickets to Dublin for $7 on New Year's Eve. We decided to go. We saw the sights, saw the museums, and of course, found ourselves in Temple Bar.

I ended up meeting a gorgeous Irish man, well call Harry, and spoke to him for the majority of the night. We exchanged Facebook and DMs throughout the night. The next day, he asked me out on a date, and Annie encouraged me to go. So I did. At the end of the night, I found myself at his apartment and texting Annie that I'd be home before our flight back to Glasgow. I received her blessing, turned on my alarm, and set my phone to silent.

We drank, we talked, we laughed, and we had amazing shower sex. And then bed sex, then the couch, and then bed sex again before passing out. In the morning, I found myself having sex with him in his foyer before probably buttoning my pants and biding him farewell. Now, I thought to myself, *I can go back to New York.*

When I arrived back, I had one night of rest before being invited out to a dance party. I went and began a normal Friday night out with my pals. I ran into Greg 2, and almost immediately a make-out session began, which led to my bedroom. We woke up the next day, and I noticed the weight he had gained since last seeing him naked, but shrugged it off and told him I had to get ready for a day out. He left, and I got back in my bed to cuddle Buttercup. I was hungover and had no plans. I decided not to reach out to him again and to stop following up with guys I'd already dated.

I was using Tinder and other dating apps pretty heavily this year. It was a roulette of men – accessible men. They weren't looking for their one and only, and neither was I. It was difficult for me to really get an idea of who these men were based on their profile pictures and what little description they'd give in their bios, but I didn't want to judge someone too harshly without giving them a chance. It was always better to meet someone in person and then make a decision. It's hard to know what a person is like through a text conversation. Sometimes they give good text game, but are horrible bores in person. Other times, they have a hard time connecting through text, but in person, they just come alive.

I decided to meet Beck, who was blond and possibly short, but I wasn't going to let that stop me. He wanted to take me to some soccer fields in Williamsburg so we could watch soccer. He brought a bottle of wine, and we watched soccer; well, he watched soccer, and I looked at the sights of the city. We saw the perfect skyline of New York from the park. I watched from sunset to where it was nearly dark out, outside of the soccer lights in front of me. I had zero interest in the game and stared more at the city than the actual field.

I typically wasn't attracted to guys who were blond and not much taller than me, but he was gaining courage from the wine and started getting frisky.

I wasn't really into him, and he wasn't very good at anything he was doing with his hands and his tongue. He was far too drunk, and he was getting sloppy. What had once been a bit of fun on what would have been a boring day had quickly slid into uncomfortable territory. I didn't want to be around him anymore.

"Hey, I've got to go."

"You're not really into soccer?"

*Or you.* "Not really." He kept looking at me, making the silence awkward. "Where do you live?"

He told me, then was silent again. Why did I feel the need to fill that silence? "Oh, I know where that is. My place is before that." Too late, I saw my mistake. I had given him precious personal information that he could latch onto and drag this disaster out.

"We can take the same cab!" he said eagerly.

"I don't know." I didn't want to spend any more time with him than was necessary, but I couldn't figure out how to avoid getting in a cab with him. He was so drunk; he couldn't tell I wasn't into him at all.

Drunk or not, he was able to get a cab, and I was stuck. "In or out," the cabbie ordered.

The car had barely pulled away from the curb when Beck leaned into me, planting his lips on mine. I had a choice. I could kiss him back and at least get some enjoyment from the day, or I could push him away and sit in awkward silence. There wasn't any harm in me enjoying myself, so I let him kiss me and gave a little effort back to him.

I was wearing a skirt, and Beck's hand shoved under my skirt, and he started pulling at my panties before I pulled his hand back and shoved him away from me.

"Get off me!" I shoved him again when he tried to grab me. I could see the cabbie looking at us through the rear view mirror.

Beck leaned forward again, and I shoved him, and he fell hard against the door of the cab.

"Okay, your ride is done," the cabbie barked.

"I don't want to spend any more time with him," I protested. "Kick him out, but I'm staying. He just tried to assault me."

"Don't kick me out," Beck moaned. "I'm good."

The cabbie pulled over. "Get out of the fucking cab."

"Beck! Get out!" I shouted, shoving him out the door. He stumbled on the curb and looked blankly at the cab as it pulled away from him.

I slumped back against the seat, almost as annoyed with myself as I was with Beck. Did I have a sign on my head that was only visible to people like Beck? Where were the amazing guys?

Back online, I matched with Benny. He was kind, and it was clear, even over text, that he was shy, but he offered to take me out to sushi, and I was always game for that.

My first date with Benny was at the most interesting sushi restaurant I had ever been to. When I walked in, I saw I had entered a curtained area. I couldn't even see the restaurant. I had a moment of panic: was I in the right place? Taking a breath to quell the panic, I moved toward what I assumed was a door, and I saw the concierge.

"Can I help you?" one of them asked me.

"Yah, I'm here to meet someone," I replied.

"Your name please."

They checked my name on a list. I hadn't known I was coming to a VIP club, but I was always up for an adventure. Once my name had been confirmed, I was directed to walk through another curtained area. The space I was now in was obviously used at night for an illegal nightclub. What was this place? The hostess was still moving, expecting me to follow her. She stopped at our table, where Benny was sitting, and I couldn't believe my eyes. Our table was sandwiched between a dance floor and a koi pond. There were panels that looked like they must light up at night, sparklers in bottles going to tables, and it was loud, with voices and music. But he was cute, so I sat. I could see the brightly colored fish swim through the water, the colors bouncing with the bass beat from the dance floor. Benny watched me take in everything with a smile on his face.

"What do you think?"

I forced myself to focus on the man at the table and not everything else around me. "I think I can honestly say I was not expecting any of this."

He laughed. "I've been told this is an intimidating first date location."

"Do you bring a lot of first dates here?" I asked cheekily. He shifted awkwardly in his chair, and I knew it was the wrong thing to say. I quickly changed the subject, but his discomfort colored the rest of the evening.

I did everything I could to lighten the mood, but Benny held himself so rigidly, he was almost afraid to laugh at any of my jokes. All the same, there was something that was so intriguing about him, not the least of which was his chosen location for a first date.

"So," I put down my glass that had once held sake, "What next?"

"What do you mean?" Benny asked, wiping his mouth on a napkin.

"Did you have anything else planned for tonight?"

"Oh." He leaned back in his chair. "Nothing particular in mind." He gestured, and a server appeared, leaving the bill on the table. I reached for my purse, and he waved me off. "Please, it's my treat." The server reappeared just as Benny pulled out his wallet, processing the bill at the table.

"Thank you," I grinned. "It was really good." I stood up and held out my hand to him. "I have an idea of what we can do."

I hailed a cab, and as Benny put on his seatbelt, I gave the driver my address. "What are we doing now?" Benny asked.

I sat back in my seat. "Something I think you'd like."

When we got to my room, I closed the door and kissed him. He was tentative at first, looking into my eyes as if he was afraid I'd change my mind. When I pulled my sweater over my head and kissed him again, his restraint faded, and he wrapped his arms around me, pulling me closer to him. I could feel his desire growing as I ground against him, and I took off my pants before falling backward on my bed. "You too," I told him, and he quickly removed his clothing, joining me on the bed. He held himself above me for some time. "Is there something wrong?"

"No. You're beautiful." He placed his hand on my breast and lightly pinched my nipple. "Do you like that?" I nodded. He moved his hand lower. "Do you like that?"

Benny was an amazing lover. He told me what he thought about my body and wanted to know if I was enjoying receiving his touch as much as he was in giving it. He was someone who connected emotionally with people. Just as in the restaurant we had the balance of my easygoing nature with his natural discomfort, in the bedroom he was balancing me out. He was the emotional connector to my desire for physical connection.

I enjoyed the balance he brought me and how deeply we connected, not just physically, but emotionally. One night, several months after our first date, when we were laying in bed after sex, he asked, "Would you be my girlfriend?"

I looked at him and laughed.

"What?" He was confused.

I sat up. "Oh, you're not joking?"

"Why would I joke about something like that?"

"I don't know. It just sounds like something a guy from high school would ask."

"Jess." He was hurt. I had hurt him, but I didn't know how to fix it. I really cared about him, but I wasn't ready for the same kind of commitment he was looking for. I didn't know if I ever would. As much as I appreciated Benny's desire to connect emotionally, there was also an element of fear. What if I gave him all of me and it didn't work out between us? What would that do to me?

He left that night without resolving anything, and I didn't hear from him for a long time. I knew he wasn't doing it to punish me; he was naturally less communicative than other people, and I didn't know what to say. It was easier to let things fade away than to be something I knew I wasn't.

I didn't know then that he would be the one I chose to get away with.

# And I'm Only 25

I couldn't dwell on Benny. I had hurt him, but I didn't know how to fix it. I didn't know what he wanted to hear from me that would erase the hurt I had caused.

It was difficult, knowing I was the cause of this rift that would become so wide it would be impossible to repair, and I didn't want to focus on it. Life was easier when I avoided the hard things, especially when I could control what I could avoid. Some things I couldn't avoid.

Once again, I found myself working at a job where I was treated poorly because of my gender. Until a woman was in a senior-level position, she typically made significantly less than the average salary of a male co-worker. I often had to hustle in addition to the day job I had, and it wasn't uncommon for me to take a sick day so I could make a hundred bucks at a friend's photoshoot. It was hard to have loyalty for companies that clearly did not have loyalty to me. I had tried to tough it out for as long as I could, but eventually, even my love for this job couldn't overcome the feelings of worthlessness my male colleagues were making me feel. I had to stand up for myself, even if I knew I was going to start the same cycle in a different position. I always had hope that things would be different, but that hope was always dashed.

After agonizing over the decision, I submitted my resignation. There was little fanfare. I wasn't the first person who was subjected to this behavior, and I wouldn't be the last. In the company's mind, I was expendable; the men were not.

While I was scouring job listings, the news trickled out that Chester Bennington, lead singer of Linkin Park, had taken his life. I grew up on Linkin Park; their music led me into my emo and goth phases and beyond into my hip-hop phase. Chester Bennington was my first crush. I knew every word of every song. I even won tickets over the radio dial in a contest as my first real concert (sorry, N'sync.) I knew every word, song title, and probably even the length of the song #CDsForLife. Shit, I even had him and Mike Shinoda on my 16th birthday cake. I drove around singing my heart out on my late nights home from work. It just felt like too much for this day where I'd just left a job that I liked a lot, with amazing people, but felt so underappreciated and underpaid. It felt like I'd done something wrong. One Thursday, mere days after learning about Chester's death, I snuggled close to Buttercup. I craved the comfort that only a beloved pet could provide.

The dark of night – despite the fact that New York never actually sleeps, seemed heavy that night. My mind didn't want to settle down, but eventually, I was able to fall asleep.

I had only been sleeping a few hours when I woke up. I didn't know what had woken me up, but I saw the door that led to the back door of my apartment had opened.

The shadowy figure of a being that didn't belong in my place came through the door. Buttercup lay beside me, her soft snores adding to my fear. Why wasn't she waking up?

The figure came closer and closer, and I was unable to move. Nothing but my head turned, and it turned directly toward the back door, which was letting in the cold fall night. When the figure reached my bed, it climbed on top of me and began to use both of its hands to push down on my chest, just as I felt strong enough to lay upward. I was unable to breathe! My heart started beating faster, and I struggled to get breath into my lungs, but everything I did seemed to aid the figure, not me, no matter how I tried to resist or fight. I tried to move my arms and legs to force the figure off my body, but nothing was working. My neck no longer worked, and all I could do was stare straight up at him… 'er it, this shadowy figure. My only option was to accept it and close my eyes. I was going to die, and I didn't know why or by whose hand.

My body shuddered, and a rasping gasp filled the room. Buttercup shifted, annoyed by my thrashing. I clumsily turned on the small lamp that sat on my bedside table – my arms felt heavy like something heavy had been compressing them. The light illuminated my room. The doors were closed, and there was no presence in my room. Had I been sleeping? It seemed so real. There was no way I could have been sleeping.

It took me several long minutes to regulate my breathing and feel safe in my room again. I left the light on, but I knew I wasn't going back to sleep that night. I had never thought much of sleep paralysis before; I'd seen some interesting articles on it, but knew without a doubt I had suffered from an episode.

I always had the feeling that I had anxiety and depression, but I thought I was able to manage it. Sure, it seemed like everyone in New York struggled with some form of mental illness, but it wasn't that bad… Was I?

I couldn't dwell on that either. What good would it do? As with everything, I shrugged it off – the fear, the panic, and the residual feeling of being suffocated and moved forward with work and life.

Dating online was relaxing at times. After a busy day at work, I could lie on my couch, open my Tinder app, and mindlessly swipe right or left. There was a limited investment, so even if I did match with someone, it never bothered me if we didn't take it beyond the initial match.

I matched with Nick after a marathon swipe-right session. He must have been online when we matched because he immediately started messaging me. When he suggested meeting at a bar that was on the ground floor of his building, I didn't have any hesitation. I couldn't identify any red flags, and I thought by this time I was adept at discerning red flags, yellow flags, and green flags.

He was covered from head to toe in tattoos and wore big, coke-bottle glasses that were too big for his skinny face. His body screamed like Avril Lavigne would feature him in a music video. I didn't know if he was suffering from malnutrition or extreme drug use, but I did know that he owned that nerdy skater vibe, and I was into it.

At first blush, he seemed weird, but not so weird that it wouldn't be a good match. He was geeky, which I had no problem with despite me not identifying with anything he enjoyed. He made me laugh, and his tattoos lent him an air of mystery, which admittedly was a turn-on for me, and most importantly, he was easy to be around.

"You're a DJ?" I asked when we were on our second round of drinks.

"I am."

"Like you mix tracks, or you click on the songs in your program?" I made sure my tone was light to soften the landing of this question. I had met men before who boasted they were DJs when, in reality, an iPod shuffle could do what they did.

Nick took the question in stride. "No iPods here." He must have heard that question before. "But you don't have to take my word for it. I have a gig every Sunday. You should come to the next one. It's tiki brunch next."

"Wait, you're a DJ, and one of your gigs has themes? Dude, where have you been all my life? Dressing up is like my favorite thing to do!"

"Then you have to come to my next one."

Our next date was planned before we were barely an hour into our first one. This had to be a great sign.

It didn't take long for me to notice that, unlike other men I had dated, Nick and I didn't do a lot of activities together. We wouldn't go on adventures; we would just go to a bar — either one he worked at, one close by, or near my apartment. We'd have something to eat, which I typically paid for. I didn't mind. I was never someone who demanded the men I dated follow archaic relationship rules, and it didn't seem to bother him either, which I took as another green flag. It was great to spend time with a man who wasn't threatened by successful women.

I also didn't think it was a red flag when we had a conflict that led to a pretty heated argument. One time he told me not to do all of this molly in front of me at once. Who was he to tell me what to do? Then I went to a party without him, and he had to pick me up because I was too high to be there. Most frequently, we'd argue at the bar when he would rather stay with his boys than come home with me, and I was the one who had work the next day. In New York, you don't give your key away as fast as you do your heart, so if he was going to stay, that meant no coming to mine. Worst of all, he'd rather stay out drinking shitty beer by himself.

He liked that I was strong-willed. Of course, Nick would only tell me that on a day we didn't have a fight. I'm sure he didn't appreciate my stubbornness in the midst of an argument, but couples fought. No one can get along 100% of the time.

Then things changed. The more serious we became, the more we pulled away from each other. I knew he was doing it, and I knew I was doing it. The separation would lead to more fights.

"I thought we were going to go to dinner." I'd say on an evening after a bailed date.

"It wasn't written in stone," he'd reply. He was nonchalant, and it didn't seem like he was hiding anything, but there was a niggling at the back of my mind. Why had he canceled? Sometimes he didn't even cancel; he just wouldn't show up, and I'd be sitting in a bar or at a restaurant by myself, trying to pretend to all those around me – patrons and serving staff that I wanted it like this. That I hadn't been abandoned.

I'd stew in the silence, and eventually, Nick would look up from his phone and catch my glance. "What?" he'd challenge.

I'd shake my head. "Nothing."

"No, there's something. Do you not trust me?"

I threw it back at him. "Should I not?"

He'd stand up in a huff, put his phone in his pocket, and leave. Sometimes he'd say something, but most times, he'd just shake his head.

I'd be left wondering why he wouldn't fight harder for me to trust him. If he was so willing to give up the argument, didn't that mean I was right to be suspicious?

I'm sure my friend Angel was tired of hearing about it, but I couldn't stop complaining about Nick when we spent time together.

"It's not just that he cancels. It's why he cancels. Like, what else does he have going on in his life that he can't come for dinner? What's he going to do, cook by himself?"

Angel snorted. "I doubt it. The man is lazier than a legless cow."

"He is, isn't he? And far be it from me to complain about someone drinking, but he drinks a lot, right? And if I'm noticing it, then that means it's really a lot!" I held up my finger to add a point. "And he moved, and I still don't know where he lives."

"Okay, but you don't actually think he's cheating or anything?"

I sighed. "No. He can barely make the time for me; there's no way he'd give up his time for a second person."

"So you don't think he's cheating, but he is lazy, and he drinks too much."

"That about sums it up."

"Is he worth it?"

I heard Angel's question repeat in my head for days. Every time hours would go by without a text or I'd get a single-word response that didn't clear anything up, I'd hear, "Is he worth it?"

I was close to coming to a decision when he called me. Right away, I knew something was up; he would never call me.

"Hey Nick, what's up?"

His voice was thick with emotion. "Jmix was murdered."

"What?"

He repeated the sentence but stumbled on the words. He was clearly upset, but I could also tell he was drunk, more drunk than I'd ever heard him be. I knew he shouldn't be alone, and I willed time to move faster so I could leave work and be with him.

I made my way to the bar I knew he'd be at, trying to call him along the way. I had sent multiple texts throughout the day, but they had all gone unanswered. I didn't know if his battery had died or if he had completely checked out, but I was worried.

I didn't see him when I got to the bar. I caught the bartender's attention.

"Have you seen Nick?"

"He's gone." The bartender was in a foul mood, I could tell.

"I realize that, but I really need to find him. It's important."

"I don't know what to tell you."

"Come on, just tell me if he told you anything."

"Why would I tell you that?" He poured a beer for another patron, ignoring me.

"Listen, you jackass, his friend was just murdered. Nick is in a bad place, and if he's not here, I need to know where he is."

"Sorry, can't help you."

I pushed away from the bar, throwing a middle finger in the direction of the bartender.

There was one more bar I could check, but if Nick wasn't there, I didn't know what I would do.

He was sitting at the bar, his shoulders slumped, and his head almost resting on the bar top.

"Nick! There you are!"

"Hey, Jess."

"Did you turn your phone off? I went to the other bar and was worried I couldn't find you."

He looked at his phone. It was clearly on; I could see the shine of the clock. "Oh." He swayed, but made no effort to acknowledge my worry.

I didn't want to be mad at him – his friend had just been killed, but the heat of anger started boiling inside me. More of his friends staggered in, and I squeezed in beside Nick as the crowd gathered to lift a glass to their departed friend. It was hours, but Nick finally stopped drinking, though that was probably due to the fact that no one was buying for him anymore.

"I don't want to go home," he said, his words accompanied by the strong stench of alcohol.

Whatever anger I had felt earlier that evening had transformed into pity, so it wasn't difficult for me to wrap my arms around him and tell him I'd take him back to my place. I'd never seen him so vulnerable before. Someone had to take care of him.

Nick didn't ask me to go to the memorial, but I went to support him and a mutual friend of ours who was also mourning the loss of this friend. Nick didn't acknowledge me to much during the memorial, as he was giving people tattoos in honor of their friend, but afterward, he and I and some friends went to a diner. Nick drank more than he should again, and I had him come back to my place so I could keep an eye on him.

For a few weeks after the memorial, Nick seemed to be comforted by my presence, and I encouraged that. If he was with me, then he wasn't doing anything reckless, and I swore he would have destroyed his liver in days if he continued the way he was.

A month after the memorial, I had to attend a fundraising event. I had been planning it for weeks, and the stress of it, as well as work and the emotional support Nick had needed, was weighing me down. I needed my own support at the fundraiser, so I asked Nick to join me.

Nick knew about the event. I had been talking about it for as long as I had been planning it, but he always seemed disinterested. As he came to terms with his friend's death, he pulled away from me more. When I left a message and a few texts asking if he would come to the fundraiser, he never responded.

This wasn't fair. I had helped him in his darkest moments. I had taken time off work for him when he didn't want to be alone. I had canceled plans with friends. I wasn't keeping score because that's what we do when we're in a relationship, but it wasn't equal either. I would drop everything for Nick, but if something didn't suit him, then he couldn't care less. I felt used. Angel's question, which had been lying dormant and silent since Nick's tearful phone call, began resurfacing. "Is he worth it?"

On another night, when Nick was silent and doing God knows what, I wandered down to my local bar. It was never quiet there, but it was comforting nonetheless. After finishing a drink and before ordering a second one, I slipped outside for a cigarette, only to see Nick lighting one up.

"Didn't expect to see you here," I said. Nick didn't respond. Fine, if he wasn't going to talk, he was going to have to listen. "It really sucks that you bailed on me with my fundraiser. You knew how stressful planning it was. You knew I needed support. I have been there for you; would it have been so bad to have been there for me?"

Nick was quiet for so long that I thought he would never speak again. Finally, he spoke, "You know Jax likes you, and he's a lot nicer than me. Why don't you just date him?"

I had met Jax when Nick and I first started dating. Nick was right; he was a lot nicer than Nick, but he didn't get to brush me off like that. I wasn't a thing to be loaned out.

"That's not how this works. You can't just pass me over to your friend because you can't deal right now." This time, I didn't wait to see if he'd respond. I stubbed out my half-smoked cigarette and went back inside for another drink.

I wasn't able to let it go the more drinks I had. I knew Nick was drinking as well, and though I knew in our frame of mind it would be impossible to have a civil conversation, I was tired of the back and forth and I wanted a resolution. I wanted him to know how shitty he had been behaving. I did not, however, want a scene in the bar, so tried to get him to come back to my place. He was not receptive.

"Come on. Just come back with me, and we can talk about all this."

"No. I told you. I'm not a nice person."

"I know it's been hard for you. I've been there for you, haven't I? Let's just talk about this somewhere that's mor…"

He held up his hand and cut me off before I could finish. I reached for his shirt to stop him, not wanting to leave things the way they were.

Nick was livid. "You know if I pulled your shirt, the bouncer would kick me out right away. If I want to leave, I'm going to leave."

"I just wanted to get your attention. You didn't even let me finish my sentence."

"Back off, Jess," he stormed out of the bar and I went home alone, muttering, he's not worth it, like a mantra.

The next morning, I woke up and found an apology text from him on my phone. He rarely apologized, and my heart softened. Maybe we could make this work; we just had to be better at communicating.

My hope was short-lived. Despite his apologies, nothing had changed. He would go days without talking to me, and he would ignore my attempts to reach out to him, but when he finally invited me to his place, I jumped at the opportunity to be with him.

It was one of the worst apartments I'd ever seen. If I didn't know better, I would have thought Nick and his roommates, who also lived in the apartment, were squatters. The only furniture in Nick's bedroom was a mattress with a single blanket. He offered me Molly, and suddenly the apartment and the bedroom didn't seem so bad.

Eventually, though, I needed to sleep, and we lay down on the mattress and tried to share the too-small blanket. I laughed at the absurdity of two grown adults sharing a blanket that was probably too small for one person. "Maybe next time I come over, I should bring my own blanket."

"Maybe you can just go home, you fucking bitch," Nick roared. Half a second ago, he had been as exhausted as I was, and now he was pinning me to the mattress, his face, mottled with rage, inches from my own.

"Get off me!" I grunted, and with strength that only panic can provide, pushed him off me enough to scramble to my feet and run out of the apartment. I was halfway down the first flight of stairs when his apartment door opened and my shoes came sailing past my head.

In the cold night air, I realized the position I was in. It was very late, and I was not sober. It was not safe for me to be outside alone. I buzzed his apartment, but Nick just yelled something indiscernible through the intercom.

I was able to call a cab, and I turned my back on Nick for the last time. The next morning, sober, I tried to figure out where it had all gone wrong. When should I have said enough was enough? Why did I continue going back despite getting the same results time after time?

I needed to be around people who actually cared about me, who didn't use me for their own gains and their own support only to abandon me when I needed support. I needed the McConnell's.

I met the McConnell's when they were visiting from Boston and immediately felt a kinship with them. They were warm, friendly people, and I felt better just being around them. It wasn't hard to convince them to move to Bushwick, and we soon became neighbors as well. Lew would make me laugh, but despite his default to dad mode, he'd always respected my decisions. It helped that his wife would often be by my side, partying till the early hours of the morning. They were like my big brother and sister, and they adopted me, a chaotic little sister who was given more freedom than they were.

After everything went wrong with Nick, I invited myself over to one of their barbecues. They hosted them every weekend when we had good weather, and I was happy to be surrounded by people who weren't as damaged as Nick was.

A friend of the McConnell's I had never met before was in attendance. Travis was a dog trainer and watcher. He was tall and blond. Blondes were never my type, but Travis was cute, charming, and he worked with dogs, which was one of my weaknesses.

Travis was also going through a divorce, and without realizing it, I had gone from being Nick's emotional support to Travis'.

After Nick, I had told myself that I would be more upfront when I felt taken advantage of by someone I was dating, but before I knew it, Travis had distanced himself from me.

What was it about me that men felt that they could take what they needed and then moved on? It had to be me, right? As much as I wanted to blame the guy, there was a small part of me that was afraid they could identify some flaw in me and use me up till I was dry.

I hadn't heard from Travis in over three weeks when he called me. I shouldn't have answered the phone, but I did.

"I need to apologize," Travis said right away.

"For what?" I played dumb.

"You have been so great and patient with me as I navigate through my divorce, but I realized I wasn't being fair to you. It's been harder for me emotionally than I had expected," Travis explained. "I do like you, but I wanted to take you out on a proper date when I was in a better place."

"I get it," I told him because that's what you say when someone says what he did. "I appreciate you saying all that, though."

"I know it's a few weeks away, but I would really like it if we could do New Year's Eve together."

"You don't want to go to Times Square or anything, do you?"

"Oh God, no!" Travis laughed, and just like that, it was like things were in the beginning. Easy. He was charming, and I was eating it up.

Yes, I would be his date for New Year's Eve. It was a simple date; we had dinner at a restaurant and then met the McConnell's and some of their friends at a bar, where we welcomed in the New Year. This was what I had been missing with Nick, but hoping to get all those times I took him back. I was looking for growth. Travis had grown.

I fell asleep almost as soon as Travis and I got back to his place after the party. I don't know how long I had been asleep when I woke up or if Travis had fallen asleep at all.

Travis was on top of me, and his penis was inside me. I had not given consent for Travis to fuck me awake – dry, deep-deep asleep. All the growth I thought Travis had vanished while he raped me. He was hurting me, and I wasn't shy about showing that, but he didn't care. Less than a minute after I had woken up, he finished inside me, sighed, then went downstairs to check on the dogs he was taking care of.

I didn't want to stay there any longer than I had to. Before I put my clothes on, I ordered a cab and left as quietly as I could so as not to alert Travis that I was leaving.

This had broken me. I became more cautious. It was harder to open up to anyone, and even harder to talk about my feelings instead of bursting out in anger.

I needed safety; I needed to know that I was in a safe place, in my place, in my own room, with my roommates on the floor above me.

It was easier not to go too deep with men; it was easier not to care about them, about what they needed or wanted. I equated shallow with safety.

# And I'm Only 26

Travis' assault on me had unnerved me. I never escalated it to the authorities, like I probably should have. I had heard horror stories of women reporting date rape, only to be treated terribly by the police and public opinion. The women would be told there wasn't anything that could be done because they had previously had sex with their partner. I didn't want to deal with that. I just wanted to forget and move on.

After my 26th birthday, I went back on Tinder. I matched with a French man named Pierre. On our first date, he was well-dressed, something that didn't surprise me. He had a stronger accent than I expected, and his pierced tongue held a ball that was too large for his tongue, which made it harder for me to understand. I couldn't help but wonder if he had too large a piercing to make up for something that he lacked.

Despite all of that, we didn't have a bad time on our first date, and he was bold enough to kiss me goodnight. He was a good kisser, though I don't know if it was aided or hindered by his piercing on his tongue.

For our second date, I invited him to my apartment for dinner and wine, which he agreed to provide.

"How about I take you to dinner?" he asked when he arrived.

"I'd rather grab sushi. There's a place down the block. It'll pair well with that wine you brought."

"Alright, we'll walk over there."

"We could just call and order and then pick up." I thought he was wanting to stay in. What was this?

"Come on, it'll be fun."

I wasn't sure how much fun walking to a restaurant and waiting for them to roll sushi would be, but he seemed to really want to.

When we got to the restaurant, he looked around the place like he was a food critic. "Why don't we just stay here and eat?"

"This really isn't a place where you do that." It really wasn't a place where I did that. The food was great, but the vibe of the dine-in place was not. It was overly bright with weird decor.

"Let's just have a glass of wine while we wait for our order. We're here anyway."

He gestured a server over, and the decision was made. I knew how long it would take for them to prepare our food, and I was determined to drink my wine before they finished so we could leave as soon as possible.

We took our food home and ate with little conversation. I had begun to regret having him over when we were at the restaurant, but this was clinching it. He wasn't even trying to impress me.

Finally, the meal was over. I cleared the table while Pierre sat, pouring himself a fourth glass of wine. This was not going as well as our first date, but I still wanted to know what he would do with that tongue piercing during sex.

Since he made the first move on our first date, I decided to make the first move here. When I came back from the kitchen, Pierre had pushed his chair back from the table. There was enough space for me to sit on his lap, so I straddled him, wrapping my arms around his neck and kissing him deeply. He tasted strongly of wine, but still he responded eagerly. He pressed me closer to him, and I felt his excitement grow.

I helped him stand up from the chair and had to steady him as he wobbled. I led him to the bedroom and helped him take off his clothes.

He fell heavily on top of me when I lay back naked on my bed, and there was far too much saliva accompanying each kiss. He spoke French under his breath while he ran his hands over my body, squeezing my breasts and my butt, but instead of winning me over, like I'm sure he had intended, I grew annoyed. I do not like the French accent, not on men and certainly not on women.

What was I doing? I didn't even like him, and now the sex wasn't worth it. He finished quickly, with me faking it right after. Pierre flopped beside me on his back, exhaling with pride. "You're very beautiful." He tapped his hands on his chest, repeating, "Beautiful, beautiful, beautiful. Shall we watch a movie?"

I should have said no. I wasn't having an amazing time, and life was short. At the same time, life was short; what was the harm in watching a movie with him? He wasn't rude; he didn't hurt me; he just wasn't great.

"Sure." I turned on the TV and flipped through the channels.

He stood up. "I'm getting more wine."

I told him I'd like a glass, and he nodded with authority. He wasn't in the kitchen long when I heard a shattering sound. I jumped out of bed and found him standing naked amongst shards of broken glass, crying.

"Did you hurt yourself?" I asked, finding some sandals to put on and grabbing a broom.

He didn't wait for me to return with the broom and began picking up the larger pieces, tears streaming down his face.

"Stop! I have the broom; don't use your hands."

Pierre took the broom from me. "I made the mess. I must clean up."

I stood there awkwardly, not knowing what to do or say, as he swept up, still crying. After he dumped the last of the glass in the garbage, he finally spoke, "My grandfather lived in Spain before he died."

"What?"

He sat down on the floor he had just cleared and began sobbing. "He was a great man, and he lived in a small villa. I wanted to visit but the timing and the weather, and I had a job."

"I don't understand."

"That's just it!" he almost wailed. "I didn't understand, and now he's dead. I will never be able to understand, and what did he think? Did he know?"

"I'm sorry," I said, unable to say anything else. "Was this recent?"

"No!" he wailed.

I was at my wit's end. His grandfather had been dead for years, and he was crying about it now? What was I supposed to do?

He looked at his hands, then rubbed his face.

"Do you want to put your clothes on?" It was absurd, this crying, naked Frenchman sitting cross-legged in the middle of my kitchen.

When Pierre didn't respond, I went back to my room to put on a housecoat. Perhaps if I led by example, I could get Pierre back in his clothes. If he put his clothes back on, maybe I could get him out of my apartment.

Pierre began speaking in French through his tears. I took my glass of wine from the table – he had dropped his own empty glass, and chugged the wine that had been left in the glass.

It seemed like hours before Pierre finally stopped crying. "I must go home."

"Yes, you do. I have to get up early." I hustled to my room and brought his clothes out to him. I didn't want any barriers to him leaving once he had made up his mind.

I opened the door and stood by it as he made his exit. He paused halfway through the door, and my heart stopped. What was he going to do now? He merely looked at me with watery eyes and a runny nose, then left without saying a word. I quickly closed the door and locked it. "What the fuck was that?" I asked Buttercup.

***

Project Parlor is one of those great bars that is off the beaten path. It's near the projects where Jay-Z grew up; he

150

actually worked at the chicken place that had given me food poisoning a few years ago. When I lived in Bedstuy, I was young, dumb, eager, and poor as fuck. So, Project Parlor was cheap, loyal, and always had men to talk to. PP was my daily, and its location meant that the price for drinks was affordable. I was often one of the few white people at the bar, but that didn't bother me or the non-white patrons. I may have been white, but I had something else in common with them – a lack of money.

It was at Project Parlor that I met Pedro. He was standing by the bar when I came in with a gust of wind – a hurricane was coming, wearing a long black shirt and black pants. For such a standard color, black was certainly making a statement on Pedro.

I was drawn to him, and even though there were multiple empty chairs at the bar between the front door and Pedro, I wasn't satisfied until I was sitting on the chair closest to him.

I had never experienced chemistry with anyone like I experienced with Pedro without even learning his name. He looked at me, his intention clear in his eyes. I didn't shy away from his gaze but met it head-on.

I waited for him to speak first, but he didn't say a word. Sparks flew between us but still he said nothing.

"Hi," I said. Was my voice husky enough, or did it scream the lust I felt for him?

He let my greeting hang in the air and just examined my entire body. I hoped he liked what he saw. "Hi."

I held in a moan. The sex that accompanied that single word was almost too much.

Pedro waved over the bartender in a casual gesture and nodded in my direction. "I've got her."

The bartender looked in my direction. "I'll take a PBR and a shot of tequila."

It wasn't a huge gesture. This was the cheapest bar in the area, but I didn't care. I wanted to fuck him.

As casually as he had waved over the bartender, he ran his fingers lightly up my arm. I was ready to jump him right then and there. "What's your name?"

"Jess."

"Jess," he tasted my name. "I'm Pedro."

I took a drink of my beer, hoping it would cool me down a little.

"What are you doing later?"

I shrugged my shoulders nonchalantly. "Nothing, really."

"Can I take you home?"

I kept my cool. "Yes." I smiled. I wanted to chug my beer right then and there so we could leave, but I didn't want to seem desperate.

When I took the final sip of the beer, Pedro took the pint glass from my hands and set it on the table. Then he took a few bills from his wallet and tossed them on the counter, catching the attention of the bartender as he did so.

"Thanks, man. Have a good night," the bartender said.

Pedro nodded, then took my hand and led me out of the bar.

He didn't seem to be walking very fast, but it was faster than my normal speed. He wanted this as much as I did. This was going to be amazing.

It wasn't long before we were at his building, but moments after he closed his apartment door behind us, my eyes began tearing up.

"Do you have a cat?"

"Are you allergic? Do you need to…"

"I'm fine," I interrupted, lying. There was no way I was going to leave this man without having sex with him. It was just some cat dander. It wasn't going to kill me.

The anticipation he had created in me at the bar meant every touch caused little bursts of explosions in my body. His hands, his tongue, his penis; I wanted more; I wanted it all the time. But his damn cat needed to give me space.

I was so satisfied after sex with Pedro, I didn't notice until the next day that even after calling me a cab and kissing me sweetly before saying goodbye, that we hadn't made plans for a second date.

I stood in the shower with that realization, trying to remember if he even had my number or if I had his. No, it was fine. We had exchanged numbers after the first round of sex but before the second one.

I refused to play the texting game some people seemed to excel at. If I wanted to see a guy again, I texted him. I didn't wait a certain amount of time or follow whatever rules some people lived by.

It was days before I heard back from Pedro again. I had almost given up on him. So he was the silent type.

"Why doesn't it bother you with Pedro when it annoyed you with other guys?" my friend Lucy asked.

It was a valid question, but it wasn't one I hadn't already asked myself. "I can't quite explain it. He's just so charismatic within the silence."

Lucy wasn't convinced, but I wasn't worried. I was busy with work projects anyway.

It had been a few days since Pedro's last text when I saw him on the subway. He didn't see me, and he had earbuds in, so I crept up behind him and clutched his shoulders. "Boo!"

He jumped, pulling out his earbuds, and turned around. "Oh. Hey Jess."

"What are you up to?" I pointed at the duffel bag he was carrying.

"I'm going camping." I knew I had told Lucy that I liked his charismatic silence, but that day on the subway, the veneer cracked. I wanted him to ask me to go with him. I didn't love camping, but I would have enjoyed it with him.

A few months later, I moved even further in Bushwick – a different neighborhood and didn't visit Project Parlor as much, and I didn't run into Pedro as often, which seemed to be the only way I could communicate with him since he stopped responding even sporadically to my texts.

Lucy would see him, however, and she told me she saw him with another girl.

"I could tell he was on a date," she told me. "Is it okay to tell you?"

I shrugged. "I haven't seen him or spoken to him in I don't know how long. I'm not sure I have any kind of ownership over him."

"Okay, so his date went to the bathroom, and he, like, immediately came over to me. He's like, 'It's Lucy, right?' and I go, 'Yah.' Then he asks, 'You're Jess' friend, right?'"

"Oh right, you guys met when we saw him at AfroPunk."

"I couldn't remember when, but I knew we had met. But listen. I told him, 'I think you knew that before you came over here.'"

I loved Lucy. She did not hold back.

"Then he asked how you were, so I said he should ask you himself."

"And?"

"His date came back from the bathroom, and he went all moody and said, 'Yah maybe.'" Lucy captured his voice perfectly, and we laughed.

"If he has a girlfriend, he's definitely not going to reach out."

"They won't last," Lucy said with authority.

I was glad she said it, but I wish she hadn't. I wanted him to text me, to call me. I wanted to be his girlfriend, not the girl Lucy had seen in the bar. I wanted to experience that night of amazing sex again.

It was weeks, almost months before I heard from him again, and I knew Lucy had been right. His relationship with that girl didn't last long. I invited him to join my friends and me at the House of Yes, an all-dance club in Bushwick. Before House of Yes, we were all going to meet at my friend Irene's to have a few drinks.

Pedro agreed to meet us at Irene's, but we didn't wait for him to start drinking and having a few lines of coke. I hadn't heard the doorbell ring, and when Pedro made his way into the living room, he looked shocked.

I jumped up, giddy from the drugs, and kissed him. "What's wrong?"

"Your nose is bleeding." He looked around the room and took in the empties and the drug trays.

"Oops!" I laughed. "I'll just go tidy myself up."

When I emerged from the bathroom, Pedro was sitting where I had been, snorting a line for himself.

Before he left my apartment the next morning, we made plans for him to be my date to a friend's birthday party, but he never showed up.

"I thought it would be different," I told Lucy. "He's the one who reached out to me this time."

"I don't know what to say, babe."

Almost as if he knew we were talking about him, I received a text from Pedro.

"What the fuck?" I said, reading it and rereading it.

"What?"

"He said he didn't want anything serious with me."

"Okay."

"Then he said he's worried I can't keep up with his lifestyle."

"What's his lifestyle?" Lucy grabbed my phone. "Like sex clubs? He went with what's her name all the time."

"I'd go to a sex club."

"You would?"

I took back my phone and texted him back, asking if he meant sex clubs. "The thing is, he'd never ask. Why do guys make all these assumptions for us?"

"I don't know."

"No, wait, I have a better question. Why am I always giving people second or third chances?"

Which led me to someone new, Alex. We had matched on a dating application not too long before rekindling with Pedro. One night, after coming in from the bar at a much earlier than normal time, I was bored and began to drink out of a bottle of wine I had at home. I was scrolling through Instagram when Alex's profile had a new share. I clicked his profile, looked him over once again, and decided to DM him.

"Hi stranger, want to come over?" I asked.

I received a quick response, "Sure."

I sent him my details, and he came over. It was not a formal date by any means, and he too had been drinking. We had both called it an early night with friends and unintentionally began talking into the wee hours of the morning. The conversation flowed like the falls of Niagara. We didn't know anything about each other and had never talked on the app outside of the Instagram profile exchange. Which I think made it easier to not care what the other thought, and in turn, we were vulnerable together. We had wild, no strings-attached, sex, and his alarm woke us up the next morning. He had to go home to get ready for his bartending shift that afternoon.

Before he left, he stayed in my room and talked to me while he got dressed. After getting dressed, he continued to talk about whatever unimportant topic it was and nonchalantly fingered me, looking me in my eyes while doing so. And I must say it was hot. Simple, respectful, and hot.

He left but came around quite often in between others. We never really tried to date, but I'd always call him between breakups or heartbreaks. And he would always show up. We'd go strong for a few weeks, then naturally we'd just fall out. But, as the pattern seems to show, they always come back.

I met a man by the time we were no more, I couldn't stand him you see, I had turned him into a drag queen, so really I couldn't stand me. Let's call him Lee. I met him on a swiping app of some kind. I was young and becoming interested in something more long term. While I wasn't sure I was ready, I was interested. We went on several amazing dates, wonderful dinners, movies and drinks, sitting by the river talking for hours and my favorite was early into our dating. We went to the Meatball Shop where I had my veggie meatballs. We then went to a Robyn night at a now closed club in Williamsburg. We had arrived early and no one else was at the bar, he ordered two shots of whiskey. I told him several times that I can't stomach whiskey and that I was too full. He peer pressured me into the worst decision of his night, I instantly puked all over the bar. I looked at the bartender like a puppy in trouble and silently begged for forgiveness. He looked back at me and then threw a towel at Lee to clean it up. Well dinners gone might as well drink my dinner. The bartender knew I wasn't drunk and asked what I wanted, I asked the price and added a $20 to it for his troubles. Lee and I got drunk, snuck into the illegal bathrooms (picture walls placed on an illegal treehouse in a nightclub) and had dirty sex – and I mean that in more ways than one. We had an amazing time every time we were together. One night we were meant to go meet his brother in Long Island, which I was elated about, I was going to meet his brother, that's a huge step. But due to work I was late, I cried and he still made me happy and then did what any good boy should, he fed me tacos. He had a husky who always ate my underwear if I left it in a place he could reach. I should have known he wasn't going to last when he showed me how he sometimes tied his dog to the roof and let him go to the bathroom up there…but I was young dumb and in like, major like. That winter he got the flu and I left work early in a snowstorm, got together the ingredients and made him homemade chicken noodle soup. I brought it to him, tucked him in after a movie and went back out in the storm and home so that I wouldn't catch the flu. Then that was it. He'd ghosted me and at this time I ate chicken so I knew it was tasty. I had no idea what happened. Fast forward a year to when I saw him on the same dating app. I swiped right out of anger and curiosity. "You've got a match" popped up. I messaged him asking what the fuck that was all about. He apologized, informed me his dog had been killed by a car, unrelated but it made me cry, and then informed me he had come out to his brother shortly after I saw him. He was now mostly into men and sent me a picture of him in drag. "How do I look?" He asked. I proceeded to give him tips on wigs and makeup tricks. Then questioned everything about myself I'd ever known. I was at a loss at what I'd done to help him achieve this realization. To this day I still don't know, but I did have to draw the line when he *eggplant emoji* asked me to join him on the prowl for men at House of Yes. I was strong but not that strong. I'd say my loss at this point, but I closed out the chat and began swiping. "You've got a match" appeared on my screen.

It was my roommate's friend, I knew it was temporary and that I wasn't all that interested in his personality, but hey I had to move on. So we hooked up a few times in secret behind my roommate's back, sometimes while he was home, sometimes not. But one night I finally went to Shane's house to hook up. When I walked in after a long day at work he was watching video tapes, VHS TAPES, of himself in elementary school plays and he was crying. I watched painfully as long as I could what seemed like hours was most likely only minutes, but I'd had it. I grabbed him and we went upstairs, did our business and he fell asleep almost instantly with his arm around me. I wiggled out, grabbed my stuff and left. That was that. I guess it's time for the next.

# And I'm Only 27

It was becoming obvious to me that I wasn't as stable as I wanted to pretend I was. I lived in a city of anonymity. I moved from one-night stands to dating, to chatting online, then having a one-night stand, and that was it. When I first moved to the city, I loved just hanging out in a small bar to see who I would meet. Somewhere along the line, we all stopped doing that. More and more people decided to stay in, get high, and chat on their phones. Men were playing video games instead of going out to bars.

I would join my friends who were in relationships when they went out, but it wasn't long before I needed more excitement than I was getting with them. It wasn't long before I was getting myself into trouble. Every night I didn't meet a guy, I'd fill the void I was trying to fill with alcohol or drugs. If I met a guy later on in the night, I'd be too drunk or high to do anything about it, which I felt guilty about. I wasn't going out to get high, or at least not solely to get high. I wanted to meet people. I wanted to make connections.

I couldn't break the cycle I had entered.

Clarissa, Sofia, and I were at Club Cobra when I noticed Chad hanging around. It had been years since the art show, but I still felt a sting of rejection. That sting made me angry. I didn't want to still be impacted by him. I had moved on. Clearly he had moved on, so why was it still bothering me?

Sofia was coming back from the washroom when Chad said something to her. She stopped, looked at me, then looked back at him. I could tell from his body language that he was trying to hit on her. What an unbelievable jackass!

"He wanted to talk about you," Sofia told me when she got back.

"Me?" This changed everything, didn't it? "What did he say?"

"He liked you a lot, and he said you hurt him when you flicked him off." So he still remembered when we had seen each other in the park, and I threw him the middle finger. Good. Let him hurt. I looked in his direction. He was still good-looking. It was easier when the guys lost their looks. "You should talk to him."

"I don't know." I wanted to, but I didn't want to look desperate. I wasn't desperate. I was in complete control of every single emotion.

"Oh, come on. He really likes you, and he really wanted you at his art show. Remember?"

Of course, I remembered. I remembered being thrilled that he had asked me. I remembered being confused when Amanda showed up at his side. What was she to him? What was I to him? I remember not being able to handle the waterfall of varying emotions that fell over me. At the forefront, I was jealous. Had that changed in the four years since I last saw him? There was only one way to find out.

I left Lucy at the bar and sat in the empty chair next to Chad. "Hey stranger."

"Jess! Hi."

"Long time," I said. Chad was calm, but maybe he was controlling his emotions. Maybe he didn't want to seem too eager. It would have been nice to see a little eagerness from him.

"It's been too long," he said. He placed his empty bottle on the bar, and I caught a scent of his cologne. Could I have been with him all this time if I hadn't been jealous and maybe a little insecure four years ago? "Should we catch up?"

The intention behind his question was clear. I looked in the direction of my friends and asked a question with my eyes. We had come to Club Cobra together; it wouldn't be cool of me to ditch them unless they gave permission.

They smiled and nodded, so I took Chad's offered hand, and we went back to my place since it was the closest.

In the four years since I had seen Chad, he had learned some new moves in that time, and I clung to him and then showed him what else could be learned.

The next morning, we lay in bed side by side. It was nice to feel the warmth of his body beside mine. "I'm going out of town for a few days," he told me. "This isn't an excuse not to see you; I just want to be clear that when I'm not around, it's not because of… anything else."

In the moments when I was awake before he was, I had wondered if I was making the right decision by going back to him. After all, hadn't I been burned before? Shouldn't I be trying something new, not the same thing over and over again? Chad saying that made me feel better about my choice. He was aware of my misgivings, and he was making an effort to alleviate them. This could work. This is what a relationship needed.

I kissed him goodbye and tried not to panic whenever there was a delay in response when I texted him. He gave me no reason to worry; he texted me several times a day when he was gone. I felt a weight I didn't know I carried start to lift off my shoulders.

Hey, you're back today! Wanted to see if you wanted to get together. I texted Chad. I saw the notification go from sent to delivered to read. I waited for the three dots that indicated he was writing me back, but they never came.

He's tired. He's just tired. I told myself. You'd be tired too. Don't read too much into it.

I was determined to be a better person than I was four years ago, so when Lucy asked me to meet her at a bar, instead of finding an excuse not to go and sitting by my phone waiting for a response, I told her I'd join her.

I was laughing at something the bartender said when Lucy swatted me on my shoulder.

"What?"

"It's Chad."

I looked to where she was discretely pointing and saw him with Amanda. What was this, deja vu? The old feelings of confusion, jealousy, and anger rose up inside me. "I can't believe this!"

I stared at him, wanting him to look over in my direction, wanting him to know I saw him there. I saw his head swivel in my direction, but his eyes didn't land on me; instead, they swept the room.

"Did you see that?" I asked Lucy. "He's making it seem like he didn't see me. The fucker!"

They left before Lucy and I were ready to. Truth be told, I wanted him to leave first. I wanted to have a tally of wrongdoings to accuse him of. I was the wronged person, and he needed to know.

He needed to know he had a gift: my vulnerability. It didn't come easy or cheap, but I gave it to him. I trusted him, and he stomped all over it.

The next morning, I was still angry. I knew he wouldn't pick up the phone if he called, but he couldn't stop me from sending texts.

I know you saw me last night. If you didn't want to spend time with me, then you should have just said so instead of leaving me on read.

It wasn't a big deal.

If it wasn't a big deal, then why didn't you tell me you were going to hang out with Amanda? Who is she to you anyway?

FFS, she's just a friend. God, you're psychotic.

Oh, I'm psychotic? I'm not the one dangling strings in front of girls' faces just so they can sleep with you.

Take some meds.

Dude, seriously?

I don't know what you want from me.

I want you to be honest. I want to be able to trust you.

Okay, but I don't want to have to tell you my every move.

I'm not asking for that!

There was a pause in his response, and I wondered if he was going to leave me on read again.

I'm sorry. I get what you're saying. It wasn't cool.

I had done it. I had said what I wanted to say, and we had a resolution.

I just wish it wasn't short-lived. After our blow-up after me seeing him with Amanda, we reconciled, but it didn't take long for his old habits and my old habits to clash. We'd fight and make up, and then there would be a short period of peace before it happened again.

I wish I was better at communicating with Chad. We seemed to only argue when we were drunk or high. I wish I could have the courage to say what I felt when I was sober. I wish Chad could have been a better person to me, and I wish I could have been a better person to Chad, because less than three years after our last fight, Chad took too many drugs and died. We would never have a final reconciliation.

Years before his death, but being upset about his attempt to break my heart again in such a similar pattern, so I called Alex. We did our typical two weeks strong, two weeks less strong, to completely fall out of our communications. No hard feelings; just time to move on.

Then I met Jamie. Jamie made me feel like no other man had. He made me feel like I could be in a relationship. He made me want to be in a relationship with him.

When we broke up, I didn't want to leave my bed. It was so unlike me. I had had many breakups before Jaime, and while there was a period of mourning or, at the very least, annoyance, there hadn't been this depression I was feeling.

It took every ounce of strength to shower some days. I could barely walk, Buttercup, something that had once been one of my favorite things to do.

This all wasn't because of Jaime. It couldn't be. He was just a guy. Yes, maybe he was the guy I thought I'd spend forever with – or if not forever, because forever is a long time, then for a lot of years.

I had struggled with stress for years, and I had self-diagnosed as being anxious with OCD. My friends knew this about me, and when I had my periods of anxiety, they knew what to do. This time, however, wasn't like the last.

"Babe, can I make an appointment for you?" Sofia asked one day as she tidied around my apartment.

"For what?" I mumbled.

"I think you need a proper evaluation."

"I know I'm fucked. Why do I need a piece of paper?"

"Because maybe you can get meds. I hate seeing you like this."

I hated seeing me like this, but it felt like everything was too difficult. I wanted to cry, but I didn't want Sofia to see me cry. In the end, I let her make an appointment, and after evaluation, I was diagnosed with bipolar disorder, anxiety, and OCD. I celebrated my favorite way with drinks, mushrooms, and art with two friends, Jack and CeCe. I explained to them that I had been right. I was broken, but I finally knew what was broken inside me. There was hope at the end of it all. There were some days that were more challenging than others. There were days I was so frustrated that I needed medication to fix me. Why couldn't I have just fixed myself without it? It took a while to balance the right combination of meds, but when I did, things seemed to be more manageable. I was able to talk about it without feeling guilty or like I was forever broken.

After my diagnosis, I made an appointment to speak with a therapist. She was sweet and didn't seem to mind too much that I never wanted to talk. I knew what had happened. All of this had been building up over time, and when Jamie and I broke up, it all bubbled over. That was it.

"Why don't you tell me about what it was like growing up?"

"There really isn't much to say. My mom was nice, and my dad was barely around. But not because he was an absent father or anything. He had a busy practice, and he worked."

"You said 'was'."

"What?"

"Is your mom still nice?"

I blinked. What had any of this to do with the fact that I was bipolar? Or anxious, or anything else?

"Yah, of course. Why wouldn't she be?" She was still so kind. Every time we talked, she told me about how she was helping some neighbor out with something. She was out of her mind, but that didn't mean she wasn't still the kind, nice mother she had been.

"And is your dad still busy?"

"Not as much. He's getting older but also slowing down for physical and mental health reasons." He was also a better communicator. We talked more on the phone these days. Before, he would usually just communicate through Mom. Maybe they did change.

"You look like you had a realization."

"I guess a little."

"Could you share?"

"I think in the past; I think I was trying to be perfect."

"And what does perfect mean to you?"

"I don't know. The typical meaning. The perfect daughter."

"And now?"

"I'm just trying to be me. If I could figure out what me is. Or what me I'm being on any given day."

We had several sessions together before she mentioned pharmaceuticals. "One way people handle what you have is through medication. I want to make sure you are aware of other options before we go that route, however."

I perked up. "No, I want the drugs."

In New York City, a therapist can't prescribe the drugs, so I found the cheapest psychologist I could find. I knew the drugs I needed weren't going to be cheap, but I knew I needed them. I craved the balance I was beginning to learn I lacked.

# And I'm Only 28

As I drew closer to my 30s, I was more reflective. I wasn't worried that I wasn't in a long-term relationship, but I couldn't help but be aware of how many of my relationships ended poorly. At the end of these relationships, the red flags seemed to be so vibrant, but at the beginning, there didn't seem to be any red flags. What was the shift? If I was aware of the shift, could I identify the red flags before I got in too deep with anyone?

In my early twenties, I was adamant I wouldn't date a guy younger than me. I would see the older women in the bars and join my friends as we identified them as cougars hunting for younger prey. I didn't want to be that woman in a few years' time being laughed at by the younger girls. Though I do have to say respect – get what you are after, ladies!

Now that I was 28, I began to question that stance. What was age, so long as the man was emotionally mature? As with everything else in my life, if it felt good, why wouldn't I go with it?

I met Paul through a good ol' fashion dating app. I have found I tend to go through phases of using the apps, then not at all. When it's not at all, it tends to be very hard to meet men. With the apps, they seem less likely to come up to you at a bar, which is a true shame. And though he was younger, I didn't hesitate like I would have a few years ago. He was a gym rat, into heavy metal music, and a native New Yorker. Native New Yorkers were hard to find. Most guys I met were transplants like I was, although I was always attracted to foreigners and New Yorkers the most. Someone who was born and raised in New York had something those transplants didn't have: their work hustle tended to be on a greater level, their knowledge and street smarts always came in handy, and there was something innately attractive about it.

Paul was also sober, something that I've never been to – well there were 13 days in Dubai, but that was due to finding out my one and only drink on day 1 of 14 was $55 dollars. I didn't let it bother me that he was sober; in fact, I treated it like a field experiment. If Paul was sober, maybe I could also be sober, or at the very least more sober than I was.

On our first date, Paul took me to a late-night tea. I wasn't much of a tea drinker, but I was always willing to try new things. Paul was in his element, telling me about the best temperature to steep different teas. This was completely new ground for me. I didn't know there was so much variety in tea. I thought you boiled water, put a bag in it, and waited for the color of the water to change.

I watched him drink the tea he chose. It was a dragon flower tea, and the bloom opened up in the water. "Isn't that amazing?" he asked me.

"I've never seen anything like it." I had chosen plain green tea.

"The legend with this is pretty cool. Did you want to hear it?"

"Okay." I didn't know how to have a conversation about tea, but his enthusiasm was kind of cute.

"At some point, a tea artisan had a dream, and a dragon came to him and told him how to create a tea that represented his protective powers."

"So now you have the powers of a dragon?" I asked. As far as origin stories, I had to admit, this was a good one.

"Maybe I do. And if I don't, the worst thing that's happened is that I paid a little bit more for tea than I typically would."

Paul and I parted ways after our tea with a promise to get together again soon. I enjoyed his company, despite the fact that we didn't drink.

On our second date, I spoke to him about drinking.

"Why don't you drink, if you don't mind me asking?" I asked.

"No, I don't mind. I'm not an alcoholic, nor do I have to worry about addiction issues if you're worried about that. It's more about my general health. When I used to drink, I was in less control, and I felt more physically awful. It took me a while to link the two together, but I soon learned that there was a connection between how shitty I felt and what I drank."

That made sense to me. "So it wouldn't bother you if we were out somewhere and I ordered a drink?"

"Not at all."

"What if I got drunk in front of you?"

"Jess, I promise it's not a big deal. I'm not about to sit in judgment of the way someone else lives their life. It's not like you judge me for not drinking, right?"

"No." I just felt deeply uncomfortable, and I realized it sharply. It was one thing to get drunk when everyone else around you was drunk, but to be drunk in front of a stone-cold sober person was something else.

Despite his not drinking, I really enjoyed Paul's company, but I didn't want to pursue anything beyond friendship with him. I had even tried to be with Alex in between dates with Paul to make up for a party bang when I needed to. But I knew there would come a time when Paul would see a part of me he didn't like, and I didn't want to feel judged for my choices. I was my own person; I worked hard to be my own person, and I didn't want to take a step back into being something for someone else.

I think Paul felt it too. We would meet sometimes for tea, where I would tease him about his tea knowledge and he would tell me about an up-and-coming metal band he had discovered, and our friendship was enough for the two of us.

I had matured; I knew when I reflected on it. A few years ago, I may have tried to change his mind. I would have worked to convince him to party with me. Now, I knew that wouldn't have been fair to either of us.

Around this time, I had fallen out with Alex and split things off with Paul. I was thinking about Benny and how he'd asked me to be his girlfriend so long ago. I still had feelings for him. When that Saturday rolled around and I was out at some dive bar with my friends, Benny texted me, asking what I was doing.

I invited him out, and he arrived shortly after. He was always quick to be loyal to me, not the other way around, unfortunately. I did truly like him, but I wasn't good enough for him. I convinced him to do drugs and stay up far too late at my friend's house. After the sun began to rise, we left and walked back to mine.

We had a lovely pattern going for a few months; he didn't pressure me or try to put labels on anything. I appreciated this, but I think he started to spend time with someone else, and rightfully so. He did a driftwood, where he just sort of drifted away from my sail, and we haven't spoken since.

It was with that maturity that I met Chase on Bumble. Chase looked like a lot of the guys I had dated. He was tall, had beautiful green eyes, pale skin, and a great personality. He had been engaged earlier in his life, which lent to a brokenness in him. It didn't bother me. We were all broken, I was probably more broken than most. His two front teeth, however, didn't match the rest of him. When he first opened his mouth wide to laugh, I almost recoiled. He might have chewed tobacco before, which caused his teeth to be discolored, but they were also askew.

Chase was not his teeth, I told myself. He was more than his teeth, and if things really hit it off with us, I could also get him dental insurance later.

Chase was unemployed due to the bar he was tending at closing, and he would spend the better part of a week at my place. I quickly was able to ignore what was going in his mouth because he really was so much more. He was funny and kind.

At a party, I broke my foot, and without any hesitation, Chase stayed with me and took care of me. He ran my errands and walked my dog for me until I was fitted for an air cast and became more mobile.

With my increased mobility, Chase took the opportunity to go back home somewhere in upstate, and I mean upstate, not just outside of the city, to visit his parents. It was the longest we'd ever gone without seeing each other since we started dating, but he was constantly texting me, so I didn't feel his absence as much.

He texted me one night, saying he was going to meet some friends of his.

I responded with my excitement for him and that I hoped he had a great time.

Throughout the night, he would give me updates about his night, allowing me to live vicariously through his activities since I was still supposed to take it easy.

Then his texts stopped. I thought nothing of it, assuming he was just having a good time with his friends. I didn't want him to feel like he had to check in with me; I was not that kind of hope-to-be-soon girlfriend.

It was very unlike Chase to go this long without texting me, so the next day I called him to see how his day went. I was bored being home and trying to take it easy. I needed some kind of human interaction.

"Hey, sorry I didn't get back to you. No one really showed up, so I had my mom pick me up, and we just stayed up late talking."

I paused before responding. No one I knew would spend hours talking to their mother. But, I acknowledged silently as I worked it out mentally, perhaps Chase did. "Oh, that's fine. I was just bored."

"How is your foot?"

"Honestly, it's feeling so much better. I'll be able to dance at the party we're going to." I had bought tickets to a very exclusive party for the two of us, and I was very excited to dress up and attend.

"I'll be back in the city in a few days. Can't wait to see you."

"You too."

On the night of the party, Chase was late, but it didn't bother me, as Sofia, Kaleb, and I had taken mushrooms, and I was happily embracing the high it gave me.

When Chase finally arrived, I was almost ready to go.

"I just got here," he protested.

"I know, but I've been here for so long, and I haven't seen you in forever."

"It was a week. I thought these tickets were expensive."

"They were." I kissed him deeply. "I just want to spend time with you."

He held my hand with one hand and, with his other, ran the back of his fingers down my cheek. "I missed you too. You're sure you're okay if we leave? You paid for the tickets."

"It's totally okay!"

"Alright, you've convinced me."

I practically jumped on Chase the moment we were back in my apartment. It had been longer than a week since we'd had sex because my air cast had made things difficult.

I fell asleep with Chase's arms around me, but when I woke up the next morning, I was cold, and Chase wasn't in bed beside me. Where was he? Why hadn't I heard him leave? Why didn't he wake me up?

I grabbed my phone and saw that Chase had sent me a very long text.

Jess, I'm sorry I had to leave. I woke up super early in the morning and had a massive anxiety attack. It scared me so much that I thought I was going to die. I wanted to wake you up, but I was also embarrassed. I hadn't told you about my anxiety, and I know you would have understood, but it's just a hard thing for me to talk about. I'm sorry. I'm okay, though, I promise.

I called him a few hours later. "Hey, I just wanted to give you some time. How are you feeling?"

"Better. I'm sorry."

"You don't have to apologize," I told him. "I definitely understand."

"It was probably everything at home."

"Yah, it's hard going back home. Everything is different."

"And I see things through my eyes now, with everything that I've learned. And I realize that some things weren't okay. Nothing bad or anything, but you know."

"Yah, I know."

"I think I just need a day or two to recover."

"I get it. I'll probably check in on you tomorrow though, just to see how you're doing."

"I appreciate that."

When I called Chase the next day, he was sick. This was my chance to treat him as well as he had treated me when I had broken my foot.

"You don't need to do that," he told me.

"No, really, it's fine. I don't mind."

No matter what I said, Chase was adamant that he could take care of himself. I gave him the space he needed, and it was a week before I heard from him again.

"How are you feeling? Any better?"

"Better every day."

"You'll never believe this, but I'm sick now too. Guess it's a good thing I didn't come help you. We'd never become healthy again."

Chase laughed. "Okay, well, I'll let you get some sleep so you can feel better and we can be in the same room again."

I recovered quicker than he did, and I was back to work within a few days, texting Chase as much as I could throughout the day.

Then I received a text. God, Jess, could you just not be a bitch for once in your damn life? I can't handle this!

I didn't know where this anger was coming from, and I was at work. I couldn't work it out here.

Just hit me up when you're ready to talk.

I thought he'd call later that day, but two days passed and I still hadn't heard from him. I was tired of the silent treatment, so I texted him. Sorry about the other day. I was just busy at work, but I didn't mean for you not to talk to me at all. How are you?

Anyone that has ever said, talk to me when you're ready turns out to be fucking crazy. I never want to speak to you again.

I stared at the message on my phone. Where had that come from? We hadn't really had a big fight; I had purposefully tried to take a step back before it got worse than it needed to be.

I'm sorry, really. Do you want to talk about it?

We've only been dating for three fucking months. Get over it.

With my newfound maturity came some self-worth. I was not going to chase someone who so clearly didn't want anything to do with me. The three months had been great, but he was right. It was only three months.

A week later, it started to hurt when I peed. When I realized I was in pain every time I peed, I tried to reason with my body. "Please no, please no!"

I had experienced this pain a few years before and quickly got tests done. I was right, though I desperately wanted to be wrong. It was chlamydia. The truth rushed to me.

Chase must have slept with someone when he was upstate visiting his parents and came back with it. Instead of telling me, he gave it to me and ghosted me, making me think I was the problem, that I was the crazy one. His anxiety attack was probably due to the guilt. How dare he? How dare he use mental health as a way to make me comfort him when it was his fault?

How were these guys able to disguise their true selves? Why couldn't I see them for what they were? I was practically 30 for god's sake! So, I defaulted I called the doctor, got medicine and after a few days, I called Alex.

# And I'm Only 29

Balancing is one of the hardest things I've ever had to do. I was working extreme hours in advertising, I was a dog mom, I was trying to stay connected with friends, go to the gym, and eat healthy. If one of those things I was trying to juggle got off track, I was a loose cannon. If I couldn't go to the gym or run for days, then I would get so mad at myself for not waking up early enough to do so. Then, I would eat nearly nothing, or I'd eat so healthily that I'd bore myself, which led to snacking.

I couldn't understand how there were some people who seemed to be able to do it all. Were they productive insomniacs? Were they popping pills? Were they close to their own breaking point? It was bothering me – the fact that they seemed to be able to do it all. What was so different about them that they could do it?

Then I saw behind the curtain. They weren't working as many hours as I was, so they could do more socializing. They didn't have a dog, and for whatever reason, they weren't out in the dating pool either. They didn't have as many friends. I couldn't compare myself to them; we were different.

I was beginning to stop the comparisons. Everyone's life was difficult in their own way; there was no need to compete.

Right before my 29th birthday, I made the first New Year's resolution I've ever made. I vowed to myself to take at least three days to respond to anyone when they made me angry. This was to be a magic solution to give me time to gather my thoughts, to sound more intelligent, and to be less accusatory and more honest.

2020 introduced the world to COVID-19. Suddenly, everyone was more kind. Sure, people were more stressed; jobs were being lost; people were moving or unable to pay rent; but everyone was there for one another. We couldn't see each other; we couldn't spend time with each other at restaurants, but there we were: separate but together.

With the end of the first COVID summer came the election. Biden was running against Trump, and no one knew if America would survive the year. Everyone was split; everyone was tense.

Despite New York generally being on the same page, there was still a lot of stress and division. People couldn't express their feelings, and they sat in their anger, angst, and everything else.

I had to deal with people who believed they were never wrong. Seemingly overnight, people I had known for close to 10 years had created drama, anger, or just straight up lied to me, and I didn't need that in my life, so I started to cut a few people out. A friendship isn't one-sided, I've learned, and I wasn't going to use what time I had while starting my own company, fostering, living alone, and whatever else I wanted to do with my time be destroyed by their behaviors.

I couldn't give the argument the three-day rule I had resolved to follow months ago. I had to accept that some people would never take responsibility.

Before COVID changed the world, I had to say goodbye to one of my oldest and best New York friends. Leah had been there since the very beginning, and now she was leaving the state. I went to her goodbye party to say goodbye to her, not to find love or anything else.

"Hey, I'm Terry," the announcement, while not loud – I was at a very crowded table, surprised me as I didn't hear him approach me. I jumped and gave a small cry of surprise. "Oh, I'm sorry! Didn't mean to scare you."

"No, it's fine," I told him, swiveling in my chair to face him. "I just didn't hear you come up."

"So I'm Terry," he repeated.

"Hey, I'm Jess," I said, raising my voice to be heard over the music. "How do you know Leah?"

He started to reply, but the friend I had been sitting beside returned, and I was distracted by her and forgot I had asked Terry a question. Before I was able to forget about our interaction completely, I found him sitting on the other side of me.

We cheered for Leah and shared more drinks as we got to know each other. His art studio was only a few blocks away from my apartment. I knew I was getting drunk, but he had a cute smile with a twist of a strange demeanor, and he had an unplaceable accent.

I found myself in a cab with him, and I invited him to the bar across the street from my place for a nightcap. I know that I had made a rule that I wouldn't sleep with someone on the first date, but as this wasn't technically a date, I don't think that the drunken sex we had counted as breaking my rule.

The next morning, he treated me to brunch, and we went back to my place for some more sex. He eventually had to leave for a prior engagement. A few hours later, I received a text from him with a picture of wine and the message, "Round two?" Terry knew the way to my heart: wine and sex.

That night, we came together, which was the first time that had happened in a very, very long time. I thought it meant something – after all, it's not often that I came at the same time as someone else. Maybe it meant we were more compatible?

When COVID-19 showed up, Terry was more cautious than others, which, while I respected, it did mean that it was more difficult to get together. I was growing tired of his reactions when I told him of my plans to hang out with friends, small intimate groups, or even my roommates, and everyone got a plus one. I had escaped to Mexico with my bestie/roommate during Fall of 2020. He always seemed to have a snide comment about how much he thought I was drinking.

Then I was wrongfully fired from a job. I contacted HR to discuss the issue of the firing, while I knew I couldn't win my job back, nor did I want to, I did have to get my remarks and feedback into HR. This I hoped would help future persons working there not go through what I had – at least while this HR team was in place. I knew I was fighting the good fight, but it was still difficult. I was vulnerable and alone, and Terry knew that, yet he did nothing to support me. Not only weren't we compatible, but once again, I found someone who clearly thought my needs were an inconvenience. I came back to New York and slapped his half-assed attempt to see me upon my arrival. Instead, I called Alex, and the pattern began going strong. My roommate Louie decided to throw a "small" get-together for Pride, which turned into a much larger party during COVID, and I wasn't quite ready. But Alex showed up casually four hours late, and I devoted the rest of the evening to him. We continued the pattern, going strong for a few weeks, then less so, and then not at all.

I decided to use some time to spend it with those who mattered most, who I could see in small groups (it was actually required in New York), and to focus on me and my writing.

When I started writing my story, I had wanted to have it published by the time I turned 30. Life doesn't always work out the way we plan.

In the years before my 30th birthday, I moved to New York, established myself in a career that chews women up and spits them out, and I've lived in New York for years now.

When I was in college, we were always told, "If you don't make it in NYC in two years, you didn't make it." That saying was what I heard every time I got a new job, worked on a new portfolio, and met a new client. It's been almost 10 years. I've made it.

I may not have found the connection in my life that led me down an aisle and put me in a house with a white picket fence, but I've never wanted the house or the white picket fence.

I have regrets, as everyone else does, but how many important life events have happened because of my regrets? If I haven't found a man to be that ultimate connection, I've found more of myself.

I am happier with myself; I understand more of myself, and I love myself. I'll keep going the way I've been going, but with more courage and more wisdom.

Who knows the stories I'll tell in a little under a decade, and I'm only 40?

# Thank You Page

A thank you to the men who broke my heart, screwed me, ghosted me, loved me, hurt me, and begged me along the way. I hope you allowed me to leave a scar on you. To the men I renamed in the book and the men, I didn't get to yet mention, removed from my memory, or forgotten, here's a cheers to you and my twenties.

A thank you to my dear friends whose names may not have been not used. Thank You, friends, You know who you are.